My Road To Viet Nam
A Personal Journey
By Michael R. Johnston

While every precaution has been taken in the preparation of this book, the publisher assumes no responsibility for errors or omissions, or for damages resulting from the use of the information contained herein.

MY ROAD TO VIET NAM

First edition. April 21, 2024.

ISBN: 979-8223033844

Written by Michael R. Johnston.

Preface

I live in Hanoi, Viet Nam. I live here in retirement, that time in a person's life when they no longer have to work for a living. Instead, live on the preparations for the future that was established earlier in life. I don't plan to leave this place except in the day when I go to meet my maker. Retirement here was well planned, well thought out, and prepared over 15 years. But how did I get to this place? Why did I come to this country? For that matter why am I in a country whose government is so different from the government of the United States and whose capital, Hanoi, at one time was the "enemy" during the period of the Vietnam War (here known at the American war)? Why am I here? How did I get here? What gave me the desire to be here?

There's no easy answer to those questions. This book is a look at my journey from 1968 as a high school senior in Shawnee, Oklahoma through July, 2015 as a retiree living as an expat in Hanoi, Viet Nam. It's not a travel log nor a war journal. It's the story of how faith and future merge to lead a person to the pursuit and fulfillment of happiness by being where God wants each of us to be.

Like any "road" we travel, we can see signposts that let us know we are on the right path. Sometimes those signposts aren't as obvious when we first travel a road, but on returning, we find them as a reminder of that first journey. Detours are inevitable in traveling. They are a temporary re-routing from our destination. My road to Viet Nam is filled with signposts and detours that made my 50-year journey amazing and, I hope, interesting to my readers.

Michael Ray Johnston

May 25, 2019

Introduction

This is not a war story! When I looked back on my life and talked with family and friends, we realized there was an underlying "thread" that has brought me back to a place I had never known before 1969. This book is a journal that marks the 50-year period between an awareness of Viet Nam and my final retirement settlement in the home of the USA's former enemy. Looking back at photos, journals, documents, and research, I saw a pattern and path that seemed to be set for me. As a Christian, I began to attribute this path as a plan that was to guide me through years of association with Vietnamese people and their plight for independence. I also saw how I might continue to be a part of being in a nation with its own rights. In the USA, the Vietnam War is often considered a war against Communism at the expense of 58,000+ American lives and untold millions of Vietnamese lives. As the decades rolled by, I was drawn to be among Vietnamese refugees and, finally, to the seat of the new Communist government of the Democratic Republic of Viet Nam. My "road" to Viet Nam allowed me to see what 50 years of independence in a country that is far from my homeland can be, no matter what form of government is the law of the land.

My story begins with my enlistment in the Army Security Agency (ASA) for a four-year stint. Why? On December 1, 1969 a Draft Lottery was drawn. My birthday (May 15) was tagged with the number 130. In those days, the Vietnam War had taken on a life of its own. Through the Johnson presidency, US involvement in the civil war between north and south Viet Nam escalated so quickly that a draft was deemed necessary to meet the demands of generals and politicians to win the war. The fight against Communism's spread into Southeast Asia, which was put forth during Kennedy's administration, had diminished as the purpose for our involvement. By 1969 more American troops were called to fight a conventional war. Politicians deemed it fair to use a lottery system to determine who would be called into the draft. With the number of 130, I was almost certain to be drafted.

In 1954 the Geneva Agreement was convened "In an effort to resolve several problems in Asia, including the war between the French and Vietnamese nationalists in Indochina, representatives from the world's powers meet in Geneva. The conference marked a turning point in the United States' involvement in Vietnam." France had been defeated in the Battle of Dien Bien Phu earlier that year. In the terms of the agreement, intelligence gathering agencies of other countries were not allowed to be in Viet Nam. At least that was how the Army Recruiter explained my reticence to signing a four-year commitment to the Army Security Agency. For two years, seven months, and 13 days I lived the life of a soldier in that far off land. But my experience was not typical. Since the ASA was not allowed in Viet Nam, we were named the 509th Radio Research Group. After a year of language training and two tours with the 509th, I was ready for more. But, thanks to President Nixon and Secretary of State Dr. Henry Kissinger, I was among the last Combat troops to leave that long fought war. My experiences during those short tours compelled me to spend a lifetime seeking to return.

When I got back home on March 8, 1973 and honorably discharged from the Army through an early out program, I returned to my hometown of Shawnee, Oklahoma. My efforts to fit into civilian life again, back to the same places, driving the same streets where I grew up had an empty ring to me. Though I sent many applications to various companies and government agencies, the doors to Viet Nam were closed. As an alternative to returning to Viet Nam, I married the last girlfriend I had while living in Saigon (now called Ho Chi Minh City). That 34-year marriage ended but the experiences and appearances of Viet Nam continued to keep the hope alive that someday I would return.

This story is about those small events ("detours") and experiences ("signposts") that kept popping up in the succeeding five decades. My hopes are that some can read my story and see that hope and dreams can come true if you are not willing to give up on their dreams and keep their hope alive. There were times I was willing to give up and try to make a life in my homeland. And I did a pretty good job at making that adjustment.

Looking back, I also saw something more than a dream of returning. Over the 46 years from 1969-2015 my life shifted six times. Those six major turns gave me rich and varied experiences, knowledge, and skills that would prepare me for a retired life in the land of my country's former enemy.

Through these chapters, two questions I needed answered before I could make the final commitment. How would I respond to the obvious differences between my life in the USA and life among Vietnamese? Would I be comfortable (safe, secure, relaxed) living in a Communist country? These two questions kept me from pursuing the dream until I could have confidence in my answers.

In 2000, I began to realize how easy that transition might be. After 27 years since leaving Viet Nam, I returned to visit in-laws and see what changes had come to Saigon. Four years later, on my second visit, I knew that living in Viet Nam would be a great place for me to retire. I made plans. I set the plans in motion. My son needed to be settled into University. I paid for a house in my in-law's neighborhood. Finally, I began paying off debts that had accumulated over a 34-year marriage.

As my fifth cycle came to a close, tragedy struck. My Vietnamese wife decided she did not want to go back to live in her homeland. I understood that. I was in the same boat. The USA had become a place different from my younger days. Politicians were ruining the country for retirees. Veterans of the war in Viet Nam were all but forgotten except for a token "Thank you for your service". For me, the USA was effectively pushing me out.

As the next cycle rose, I found myself in Bangkok, Thailand living with a younger Filipina who would later become my wife. On January 8, 2008 I left my son and my country to live and work out my final days before retirement in Asia. I even tried to justify that Thailand was as good as Viet Nam. The house I had paid for in Ho Chi Minh City (which was given to my ex-wife in the settlement) meant I would have to start from nothing, since all of the retirement plans I had in place for a comfortable retirement were given to her in the settlement.

For seven years I tried to assimilate into Thai culture. But nothing seemed to work for me. I enjoyed the life of a teacher again, but it wasn't enough. Organizational politics reared its head and I was too close to retirement, i.e. too old, to look for more work. I took an early Social Security retirement in 2012 at 62 years old.

Over the next three years the threads of returning to Viet Nam began to appear. Looking back over the years, the seeds of this book began to take root. All that I had done, learned, and tried were a foreshadowing (again, signposts) for the moment. I didn't know it, but I was ready for the next, and hopefully, the last cycle.

This story is a journey of faith. I hope to tell tales of that faith being tested. In this account of one man's life are the lives of people that I know who have given up faith in themselves. Without that faith in yourself, fears will push you into a life of resignation, desperation or, worse, deprivation. For some, their faith in God sustains them through their misery. They even become comfortable in their nest that was built on broken hopes and dreams. Faith in God and faith in self will build courage to overcome obstacles that fracture or break the hopes cast by a weakened faith. God promises us eternal life with him if we accept that faith as his gift. I have learned that faith in God and in one's self promises the fulfillment of hopes we have. Out of the hope comes dreams that can finally come true.

Moses led his people through the wilderness for 40 years. His faith remained focused on God's will though he never knew how long or where that faith would lead them. He held on to the faith that never leaves us. When he reached that Promised Land, he was not allowed to enter in. His faith had been rewarded by going into the mountain to never be seen again. This journey through my 40 years between 1969 and 2009 has been an exciting revelation of faith for me. The faith that I have held onto for five decades was the heartbeat that led me here. But faith in God and in myself has also been strong enough to overcome the tests that are inevitable in anyone's life. As I approached the completion of my journey, as the end of the road seemed to appear, I quietly disappeared in some ways into the mountains of Northern Viet Nam to live out these days in peace and happiness.

Michael Ray Johnston
May 25, 2019

Prologue

Michael Ray Johnston, son of Ralph Johnston, Jr. and Mattie Sue (Ivey) Johnston, was born on Monday, May 15, 1950 at 5:15 am. Anyone interested in numerology can figure that one out. In 1950, the USA was on the cusp of the coming Cold War. As I grew up in Shawnee, Oklahoma I remember the Atomic Bomb Drills – "Duck and Cover!". Families were thinking about when and how big to build their bomb shelter.

Despite the overriding fear of nuclear war, there was also great hope. World War II was a victory against Hitler's evil and Japan's aggression. The USA was recovering from the cost of that World War II. American GIs were coming home to piece their lives together and build their lives and family. The government instituted the GI Bill which gave military men and women opportunity to get back into the stream of American life once again. In Southeast Asia an era was ending, colonization was drawing to a close as France tried to regain power over their former colony, Indochina.

Dad was a US Navy engine mechanic. His ports of call were all in Asia. Shanghai was the only one he ever talked about. His gruesome story of seeing a head bobbing past his ship as they entered Shanghai's harbor told me I wouldn't be talking much with him about his War experience. In 1949 he married my mom. Later in my life, I discovered my Uncle Riley Ivey, had served during the Korean War. Though not a part of my memory, I learned that Dad had volunteered to go to Viet Nam for six months as a civilian to work on jet engines. A decade later, Mom and Dad's only son would be heading to Viet Nam. I could say that Asia was deep in my family roots.

By the time the 1973 rolled around I was on my way back to a life in the USA with a foreign born wife and step-son. I worked in a variety of professions. I was slowly and with some certainty being molded for a greater destiny. My journey might be considered a series of stops along the way to learn something new, apply lessons from my past, and prepare for a life that has been peaceful, happy, and filled with the love that matters from family and friends. This is what this story is about.

Chapter 1 - Stepping on to my road to Viet Nam

In the beginning!

At the beginning of 1969 I had no clue what, where, or why America was in Viet Nam. On December 1 I began to be aware that even if I was ignorant of the facts, May 15 (my birthday) was drawn as the 130th group who could be drafted. I quickly estimated that around July 1970 my group would be sent that draft letter to report for induction into military service. I could let it happen, be drafted, and, more than likely, be wounded or killed in action in the long running American involvement in the war over there. Or I could run away, like so many others, to go to Canada or go underground. Or I could go back to University and receive a deferment. Whatever the choice I made, Viet Nam came into my life.

I didn't dwell on the implications that number 130 would have for me. After high school, in September, 1968 I headed off to Oklahoma State University (OSU) in Stillwater, Oklahoma with my 1967 GTO loaded with the things I would need for my first year of University. I did love that car! It was, above all things, the perfect possession of an 18-year-old high school graduate to hit a university campus. I did the whole process: pledged Sigma Phi Epsilon fraternity, established a Chemical Engineering degree plan, and settled into the fraternity's lifestyle. Viet Nam was not even on my mind. Being enrolled as a student allowed me a deferment. I was also, more or less, independent for the first time of my life. Even though mom and dad were paying for that first year, I was able to make my own choices and enjoy campus life to the best of my ability. Though there was little I knew about college life, I was a fast learner. The fraternity helped to put aside being a good student and begin learning what a good learner can discover in between classes. Frat parties, drinking "purple passion" and meeting a new genre of women on campus was a revelation for me! In retrospect I realize that introduction to life outside of high school would help when I get into the swing of life as a soldier. With all the parties and distractions of campus life, my grades suffered. Fraternity life was also a burden to bear. The hazing and, sometimes, stupid and demeaning pranks of the members quickly pushed me to leave the fraternity. It just didn't suit me. That meant dorm life for me, since freshmen were not allowed to live off campus. Suddenly, I was in another new world living in a big apartment building (dormitory) with hundreds of men. I was bewildered in more ways than I had experienced in the frat house. At the fraternity, we had shared rooms for study, a dormitory for sleeping, and shared a toilet with the entire floor. The dormitory was much the same but with hundreds, instead of the 30 or so fraternity population, which was spread over three buildings next to each other. I didn't know at the time, but the fraternity and dormitory were much like the Army barracks I would be sharing in the future. At the end of the first semester, I went back home for the Christmas holidays and recovered the lost sense of home life, which wasn't much to speak about. When I returned home, I was told my sister, Patty, had been placed in a state-run facility for mentally retarded individuals. Patty was born in 1953 with a hole in her heart and afflicted with Down Syndrome, a mental capacity that doctors told our parents would not allow her to have a mentality greater than a ten-year-old mind. My younger sister, Sheryle, is 11 years younger than me, born in 1961. With only three in the household and Patty about 50 miles away in Paul's Valley, home life was a bit off balanced. Added to this home life that I never felt comfortable with, was an accident that brought a shift in my future.

During the Christmas break, my nose began bleeding. What seemed like a simple nose bleed, resulted in a rush to the emergency room. The bleeding wouldn't stop. Lying on the narrow Emergency Room table, while Mom was consulting with the doctor, I, somewhat dizzy by the loss of blood, had two things happen. First, I asked for a pan because a nausea set in and that I was ready to expel. I filled the pan with all the blood that I had swallowed during my ordeal that night. The next thing that happened, while the doctor and mom were talking about what to do next, I rolled off the table, onto the floor and broke my jaw. I woke up in a hospital room with my jaw wired shut. My stay in Shawnee, that was expected to be only the two weeks during the break, ended up being a month at home recovering enough to get back on campus.

Time away from the first couple of weeks after the semester began, gave me pause to think about what returning to campus would mean. Coming back on campus, living in the dormitory, and, generally, not excited about being back on campus, my dad told me that I would need to find a job to pay for the next semester. Dad had not planned more than one semester of school for me. I wondered if he didn't have a clue how expensive school would be or if his gift of the GTO was a way of saying "sorry". Returning to OSU, I immediately found a job pumping gas at a DX gas station on the city limits of Stillwater. It was there that I got to meet friends and others who were on the way to the lake for the weekend, while I was stuck at work.

My work ethic had been planted early in my life. First was newspaper delivery boy in a small town north of Shawnee. Dad was the Chief of Police in Meeker, Oklahoma. When we eventually returned to Shawnee, I began working at the Shawnee News Star pressroom where papers were printed, inserted, and distributed. Working from midnight to 4 a.m. before heading off to school got me familiar with coffee and sleep deprivation. When University living conditions changed, I was somewhat prepared to do whatever it took to get the job done, which included classes, pumping gas, and homework. Not much time for anything else. Near the end of the first month of 1969, I dropped out of university and began looking for work that had some value.

The first truly independent decision I made was to find a job with the State Welfare Department in Oklahoma City, about 90 miles away from Stillwater. Since my dorm room was paid to the end of the semester and the price of gas was cheap in those days, I made that daily 90-mile drive to Oklahoma City in my GTO quickly. I would head out in the morning to get to Oklahoma City by 8 am to start the day's work. That commute only lasted a short while before I moved back home for a shorter, 40 miles, drive to work. School was over for the time being. The 105 Audit Unit where I was working was stimulating in many ways. Being a part of the regular work force, I began to enjoy the environment. In future generation's terminology, it was a "target-rich environment". Ladies were everywhere. Life was moving up and I was getting to know the lay of the land quite well. The work itself was also interesting. Computers had entered the Welfare Department's data storage needs. Coming from field offices all over the state were forms that needed auditing for correctness and accuracy of cases being handled. The audit prepared the forms to send to the Data Entry unit where they would be entered into the computer. For me that meant reading a lot of case files, verifying data, and collecting interesting (non-work related stories) of clients and their lives on welfare. Between dating and file reading, I was having a great time as a single guy.

In February 1970 I met Irene Linda Garcia at the State Welfare Department where both of us worked. I invited her to be my date for the Credit Union's Annual dinner in March. By the end of the evening her bra was on the floor of my '67 GTO and, well, you know! May 7 we had a simple church wedding at her family's Nazarene Church. Everything seemed in order. Linda and I were having a great time living in the trailer house in the back yard of her mother's house.

But Viet Nam was weighing heavily on my mind. Almost daily I was following the draft lottery to know which number was being called up. Since I was no longer in college, my school exemption was withdrawn. Shortly after marriage, I visited the Military Recruiting Office and was convinced to sign a four-year contract in the Army Security Agency. The recruiter convinced me that ASA soldiers were not allowed to be in Viet Nam because of the "Geneva Conference of 1954". My naive 19-year-old brain believed him out of pure ignorance of anything with the words "Viet Nam" in them. Looking back at that road, it never really meant much to me at that time when thinking about Viet Nam. Even signing the contract for four years with the ASA wasn't a worry since the recruiter convinced me I wouldn't be going to Viet Nam. The country still seemed only a 6 pm TV news article. The only change that I could envision was travelling to places around the world where ASA was allowed. Getting that travel paid for by the government for both my new wife and I made it an even better deal.

Born into a family that was mostly dysfunctional I learned how important friends are. Living with a sister who was mentally and physically handicapped, I learned about love and being compassionate. But it would take many years to refine those emotions. High School emphasized how friendships can last a life time, no matter how long or far apart friends may be. Life, itself, is lived with a desire to reach beyond the lines set by others. Living among people who were of different colors, status, and social standing, taught me that everyone has value, no matter who they are, when they were born, nor where they come from. God's plan for my life was being played out without my knowing. Only in reflections of my past do I realize how little control I had over my life and how that lack of control has made me a happier, better person.

Did it prepare me for Viet Nam? Neither did I have a desire nor a clue that was where I would end up. My Road to Viet Nam was in "the womb" waiting to be born. I was just passing the signpost by going into the Army. There I would find new challenges and adventures that would set the stage for a life among Vietnamese.

The Road Widens

The news that I had enlisted in the Army put a strain on my new marriage. The delayed entry program meant I wouldn't have to report for basic training until August that year. Those three months of marriage prior to Basic Training in Ft. Leonardwood, Missouri were silent about the war and focused on getting to know each other. Before induction there was paperwork and administrative tasks that needed to be completed. Since I was married, even if only a few months, there was housing allowance, ID cards for both of us, marriage allotment, and, survivor forms. If I died while a soldier, my widow would be taken care of. That wasn't very comforting. As the day approached to "ship out", I arrived at the recruiting station, was inducted there, and bussed to Basic Training Camp with the rest of the recruits. That meant I would have said my goodbyes there in Oklahoma City.

Next stop, Fort Leonardwood, Missouri to learn how to be a soldier. Basic Training was eight weeks in the heat of that Missouri summer. Every day of training we heard "Viet Nam" mentioned in one way or another. I was the only ASA recruit in my company. Mentioning my recruiter's words never left my lips. The men I was training with were draftees, volunteers (like me), and criminals who were given the choice of Army time or jail time. The training did a good job of making us ready for fighting. But there was one more lesson that wasn't a part of the training course of living with men from many segments of American life. The first part of the movie "Platoon" was a reminder of what barracks life was like and how different it was from dormitory life. Waking up at 4 am to the sound of trash can lids, drill sergeants barking orders, and being called a variety of names except for the three I was given at birth was a shocking experience that prepared me for the days when getting out of bed aware of what's going on would matter.

During those eight weeks, we spent two days testing our skills and abilities to determine what each man's AIT (Advanced Individual Training) would be. At the end of those weeks, we received our orders for the next level of Army life - AIT. Mine? Vietnamese Language (Northern Dialect)-47 weeks! All I could think of was how could that be so, especially after what the recruiter told me!

October was graduation. I was promoted from Private Michael Johnston to Private First Class (PFC). The Army loves titles and acronyms. Linda drove my GTO from Oklahoma to Missouri to attend my Basic Graduation. The drive back to Oklahoma was long and silent. The impact of my AIT was numbing to both of us. My classes wouldn't start until November, but there were things we had to take care of before I began. We drove to El Paso, Texas to look for off-base housing. There were more forms to complete at the admin office. We stayed those few days in guest housing on Biggs Field, near where classrooms were. During those few days in El Paso the tension finally broke. Linda told me of her liaison with an old boyfriend while I was in Basic and she felt she couldn't handle being a widow if I was going to Viet Nam. By the end of that trip, she had decided she would file for an annulment when we got back to Oklahoma. I didn't recognize what the impact was for me at that time. But Viet Nam had taught me the first lesson in life (later I would title these moments as LiL) -the first of many in the years ahead. Hopes and dreams are wonderful things to have. In my mind I was already beginning to think of a house, kids, and a life filled with love. Even when I realized I was going to Viet Nam, I dreamed of coming home and starting that life. But we were too young. The annulment was quick, cheap, but not painless. It hurts to have love broken so young in life after tasting the wonder of it. Hopes and dreams will shatter if they are not the ones meant to be.

Getting those orders to report to the Defense Language Institute (DLI) was just a bump in the road that I did not understand. I loved Linda, but it wasn't a two-way road. I learned the hard way that love, true love, is when two people meet on that road. There is a bond that will not be broken, unless that love dies. It did. I would report to Biggs Field on Fort Bliss in El Paso, Texas alone. Getting on my road to Viet Nam was a sad story of love lost. But it was a beginning of a love I had not met yet.

You're in the Army Now

*A journey of a thousand **miles** begins with a single ste* (Chinese: ◇◇◇◇◇◇◇◇)

As the November report date approached, I loaded up what belongings I had into my GTO and headed West as a single man. The first day of class was the first time I met real Vietnamese people. All of our teachers were citizens of Viet Nam. In some way I didn't feel much of anything. I was emotionally numb from the annulment at the end of a six-month failed "marriage". A year in training was going to be a metamorphosis for me. Vietnam School would fill my weekdays and a soldier in the border town of Juarez, Mexico would fill my nights and weekends! During that year in El Paso, Viet Nam was not a country or war; it was the teachers who were helping us learn their language.

Looking back on my introduction to my journey to Viet Nam, I can't help but remember Israel's journey through the wilderness. Because of the skepticism and rebelliousness, God sent them on a 40-year journey through the wilderness. He fed them, clothed them, and made sure those who were too young to remember their slavery in Egypt were grown. The few who remained faithful to God succeeded in entering the land God promised them. In 1970 I became aware of Viet Nam as the war (technically called a "police action") that the US was involved in. That war created a lot of protest and division in my country. I had no idea what the future would be. The only comfort and assurance I had in those days was my faith in God. It truly was by faith born of ignorance that pushed me into the path that God has always promised his people: Peace. But I didn't know that I would have to wait more than 40 years for that Peace to be realized.

In the succeeding segments of my 40-year journey I give an account of God's hand in my life. That hand guided me, nudged me, directed me down alleys, lanes, roads, and highways that would prepare me to live and work among the Vietnamese, travel in their land, and learn to call that far away land, home.

If I was made aware of Viet Nam, the country, in 1970, my introduction to Vietnamese people was surely in 1971. I arrived in El Paso early in November 1970 to be introduced to my teachers who were native speakers of the northern dialect. I didn't know, nor was I interested in when or where, in Viet Nam, they had come. All I knew or wanted was to discover El Paso and finish the 47 weeks of language training. It wasn't that I didn't like studying language. After all, I had been the President of my High School Latin Club. And I had a fairly good grasp of that ancient, dead language. But Vietnamese? I tried not to think about graduation, but I did take an interest in the new language. Watching them teach us was an exercise in a world I never imagined for me-teaching English to Vietnamese! But that would be decades ahead. The days in Texas were filled with anything and everything to take my mind off of my final destination. I had joined the Army Security Agency (ASA) because I was led to believe that ASA was not allowed to be in Viet Nam.

As I entered the classroom and greeted and joked with my teachers, I was moved by their commitment and marveled how they seemed to successfully hide their true feelings. It was Mr. Anh that "spilled the beans". Not in word did he express his feelings nor what he was thinking. It was his break times-those moments when he was not teaching or was outside just before he had a class. One day I saw him walking with a stick in his hand. He was just stirring up dust and whacking rocks. But his posture suggested he was deep in thought. I wondered what he was thinking. Was he homesick? Did he have a problem teaching men who would be following the movements of his countrymen which would lead to their death or capture? Watching him was all I did, never to invade his thoughts, nor question him of why he was there in El Paso. Being introduced to those teachers was a revelation for me. I didn't know it at the time, but watching them try to teach us and seeing them talking among themselves started me thinking about the motives behind someone who leaves their homeland to live and work in a foreign land. I would be making that move in a year, though it was not by my choice. My thoughts leaned to thoughts about living in Asia! My doodles during class were strings of words thrown together for the thoughts that crossed my mind about living outside of my homeland.

Language training was not the only revelation and change in me while living in El Paso. First, there was living outside of my home state, Oklahoma. After Basic Training at Fort Leonardwood, Missouri and the annulment, I was ready for a better change in my life. Oklahoma was "home" in name only. There wasn't much reason for me to stay there. I didn't know what I wanted to do nor where I wanted to be. I only knew Oklahoma didn't hold much interest for me. The year in OSU was a failure, family life with mom and dad was depressing, and, of course, losing at my "first" love was something that was hard for me to manage emotionally. The best I could do was to go wherever the Army sent me.

When I got to El Paso, I joined a bunch of guys who seemed to feel the same way. There was one who felt strongly about leaving his hometown. He shared with us that he was tired of what he faced at home. He wanted adventure and new sights. He wanted a world where prejudice was not so hurtful. So he joined the Army and ended up with us in Vietnamese Language Studies in El Paso. The only problem he had was that his hometown was El Paso! 1971 opened doors in my mind to let seeds that were planted during my days at OSU sprout. Those seeds were nurtured by living and working with people I met while in Oklahoma City after leaving OSU. Jan, Amelia, Penny, Jean, Connie, Diane, Cynthia, and a few others who were a part of my life that had meaning for me. Not in a relationship way, but as teachers of a sort.

We live our lives in communities. We step outside those communities and find something else that expands our horizons and teaches us about being and doing things with others. In a 2017 movie, "The Arrival", the linguist tried to explain the importance of learning the meanings of the Alien's language and bring into play what our language means-a universal language. It's not unusual. It's been tried often enough. These days, English is a language that is spoken as much or more than Chinese or Spanish. Two thousand years ago Greek was the language of the day for business and, to some degree, science. Latin later became the "franca lingua" in Western Civilization. But it's not language that is the substance of understanding. Language is simply the vehicle that brings us together. The story about the Tower of Babel records a universal language that was misused. Man's arrogance and his desire to rise up to God created the separation that we have been dealing with for eons. The people in my life are not teaching me new languages, dialects, or cultures. They are teaching me how to communicate with others to understand what allows peace to infiltrate barriers and resolve differences. That was 1971. I was surrounded for almost one year by people from different American backgrounds, the different cultures and social surroundings of life in America. Language school added contact with people from a completely different nation, culture, and society that was involved in war. Army life was my next classroom. Next to our barracks were Army Rangers. Our daily walk past their barracks brought jeers thrown with laughter and the same arrogance found in the days of Babel. Every weekday

I was in a classroom and taught by men and women from across the ocean in Asia. A step across the river and I was in Mexico. My lessons in life were becoming an international awareness.

In 1971, I was beginning to discover who we are as people under one environment, Earth. How did that affect me? In my unconscious mind I was assimilating one little corner of this massive world of billions of people. For the years ahead, that notion was planted and took root. Little did I know that within each of us is a conduit of understanding as long as we can come to an understanding of what we mean and what we intend to communicate. For the next 40 years I would be on a journey that ultimately led me to this country I now call home, Viet Nam. In the succeeding years from the end of 1971 through March of 1973, I would be transplanted and thrive in a nation and culture that I had no knowledge of before that time. I recall a group of people who were driven out of their suffering into the hands of a people who were not theirs. Through the leadership of one man they left their bondage to begin a 40-year journey that was not planned nor expected. I was on my journey through a wilderness, an uncharted wondering, that would take me to many undiscovered territories.

A Brave New World
"Goooood Morning, Viet Nam"
Robin Williams as **Adrian Cronauer**

By the end of 1971, I was single and settled into the barracks at Biggs Field on Fort Bliss in El Paso, Texas! Though surprised by the sudden end of my marriage, I somehow knew things would work out, not to be married again, but to realize that in some way my road to Viet Nam was a part of that bump in the road ahead. I really didn't know how much the drive to El Paso would mean to me until decades later. But I drove down that long highway from Oklahoma City to El Paso in my GTO with an open mind and free spirit.

The first day of classes was more a matter of orientation than understanding where those studies would lead. It's ironic that the venture into ASA would take me where I did not want to go – Viet Nam. I didn't complain, argue, or protest. Instead, without really knowing at that time, I simply let things happen. Over the years I discovered that such a philosophy has given me a peace of mind that is very hard for some to understand. Looking back on the times when I have followed that course, my life has been exciting, inviting, and provocative. New avenues that I would not have known about are opened. By the time I got to Biggs Field I had put the idea of going to Viet Nam into the back of my mind. Instead, I felt a sense of curiosity. What is that place, Viet Nam?

Meeting my teachers was the first time I had ever met someone from that country. The Defense Language Institute knew how important learning a language from native speakers was. They had recruited Vietnamese who were native speakers of the Northern Dialect. Seeing them as teachers instead of people who spoke the dialect of those that Americans were fighting didn't enter my thoughts. Learning the language was not to know what the "enemy" was saying but to me, learning the language was travelling the road I would discover later in my life.

The Army recognized that my ability to pick up a language was better than most. My talent had shown itself in Shawnee High School. In those days, high school required credit for a foreign language. Rather than the typical language of Spanish, I elected to take Latin! Later, in the 1980's, when I attended Seminary in Texas, I was also introduced to Ancient Greek and Hebrew. While I was in El Paso, I even took two computer languages (COBAL and FORTRAN) at the University of Texas, El Paso.

There wasn't much motivation to learn Vietnamese. That is to say if I learned it well, I would be going to Viet Nam for sure. Where that would lead me was not something I would dwell on. But I took the challenge to learn a new language and, with that purpose in mind, I chose to enjoy the year I had in El Paso. Military life in an Army base town and close to the border of Mexico offered many nights and weekends of adventure to be explored. If I had been more aware at 20 years old, I might have realized I was learning a philosophy of "things will work out."

Looking back there were many experiences that introduced me to new ways of thinking and acting that would affect my life in the years ahead. Studying in DLI was much like being in a University, except that the students wore uniforms and were being trained for use during war times. The teachers spoke English with an accent that was new to me. They were citizens of another country, and were there to help their country, South Viet Nam, overcome the "communist aggression" from the North. Among my teachers there were two, Cô Thuy and Mr. Anh, that were especially memorable. Cô Thuy was a beautiful lady who made heads turn. Her professionalism made her even more admirable. Of course to a 20-year-old who had loved and lost just weeks before, she was a dream come true. Not that there was any hope of getting to know her better, I did enjoy the classes where she was the teacher. As she sat behind that desk or stood at the chalk board to explain that new language, my mind strayed often enough to wander what she must have been like when she lived in Viet Nam. Mr. Anh was a man of mystery. Not in a bad way, but as someone who kept to himself. The one moment from all that year of classes, I remember one day during break-time, he was alone, outside with a stick stirring up dust and seemed to be in a thoughtful moment. He seemed sad but he never seemed to bring that into the classroom. Again, his professionalism was making an impact on me that I did not recognize until decades later. That impact was focused on the way each teacher took their position seriously as teacher. Perhaps it was because they had decided that teaching these young men their language would in some way help their country find peace in their land by ending the war sooner. For me, their presence and teaching were the introduction to a people and culture that would come to the forefront of my life four decades later.

Then, there were the times away from class. A GI in a border town was an open door to party life such that a boy from Oklahoma had not experienced. Juarez, Mexico was a short walk across the bridge over the Rio Grande that separated the USA from Mexico. With our Military IDs safely tucked away somewhere in our clothes, we often ventured into the stereotypical Mexican border town of Juarez. Bars, girls, food, and souvenirs of all kinds of distraction were for our enjoyment. Bars like "The Cave", girls who would "give a show" for $5 from each GI who wanted to watch, or the food that was the real Mexican cuisine, not the Taco Bell fast food. Souvenirs were not just the three-quarter length, leather-fringed vest I bought, but a few "souvenirs" that would require a shot of penicillin to help keep me healthy! The stories are many, but the time away from class was an education of a world I never knew existed. One that I would find to be prevalent down the streets and alleys of Saigon.

There was one more education going on that would make my road to Viet Nam a little bit more interesting and enlightening. In my spare time I took advantage of the Crafts Shop that most military bases have available. Since my days in High School with buddy Tom Catlett, our Yearbook Photographer, I had become very interested in photography. In high school I had my instamatic camera! In the Army, there was a darkroom where I could learn the basics of processing film and making prints. In the Base Exchange, I bought my first "real" camera – the Yashica Mat 124. It was a nice big film format (6x6 cm) to develop an eye for imagery. Once I got to Viet Nam, that one experience would take me out of a combat area and safely entrenched in the wiles and ways of Saigon life in the years that followed.

El Paso was more of an awakening to the world at large. Foreign countries, loose women, good times with buddies, and a language that would ultimately take me into a foreign conflict. As 1971 came to an end, new thoughts began to take shape. My orders were to report to Travis Air Force Base near Oakland, California. Those same orders directed me to report for orientation and transfer to the 8th Radio Research Field Station (RRFS) in Phu Bai, Viet Nam. I had heard that it was so close to the De-militarized zone (DMZ) that the North Vietnamese flag could be seen flying. I was given a few weeks after graduation to get my affairs in order before heading off to the war. The adventurous days at El Paso: the Levee, the classes, the border town, the memories would be left behind.

Over the years there are opportunities to visit the world at large. I have read somewhere that less than 10% of American Citizens have a passport! We are a people living in a country that is so vast, there doesn't seem to be a desire to step outside of our borders. People from other countries, cultures, religions, and societies visit the USA with wonder and curiosity, but Americans, too many perhaps, take our amazing land for granted. As beautiful and diverse as it is, there much to be learned by stepping across those borders to see the world. After a decade and meeting many "expats". I've realized that crossing that homeland border changes us. Travel, whether across a county, state, or country is an education in itself. An education that is filled with risks which can mold attitudes that we carry with us. El Paso was my first stop on my Road that introduced me to "foreigners" and countrymen alike to teach me that all people are the same in some ways yet, also different in many other ways. Meeting with people from other places, cultures, societies broadened my world view and helped me to embrace human kind with a hope for being a member of a greater world of people.

The next leg of My Road to Viet Nam would be my first visit outside of my United States of America. Was I ready?

Chapter 2 - Arriving in Viet Nam

The door to wonder is through the windows of the world

On the Wings of Northwest Airlines (Nov 1971)

November 5, 1971. After the 14-hour flight by Northwest Orient Airlines, I stepped off the plane onto the tarmac at Bien Hoa/Long Bien airfield, just a few miles north of Saigon. Arriving at Bien Hoa airport was my first experience with tropical heat. De-boarding the plane we walked across the tarmac to waiting buses where troops would be shuttled to departure zones according to their orders. The first step out of the plane was a wave of humid heat that would be the mark of the new world I had entered. Decked out in my brand new jungle fatigues, like everyone else on that flight, I was as new as any "newbie" could be. Did I have a clue about what I was in for? Or any expectations for this next year? Not a bit!

I walked off that plane totally oblivious to the dangers that were before me. Neither scared, anxious, nor worried I simply did and went to where I was told. I accurately remember that moment on the bus waiting to be taken to the truck transport. I sat in the back row. My shirt sleeves were rolled up. My hands rested in my thighs as I watched a bead of sweat form on my forearm. I watched it grow into a bead big enough to, finally, roll down my arm. That was all I was thinking about, that bead of sweat. Looking back, I seem to think that was the beginning of my philosophy of thinking only in the "now". These days, it's a psychological exercise to relieve stress. Back then it was just thinking about that drop of sweat and how long it would take before it began its fall.

Boarding the awaiting bus that would take us to a waiting "deuce and a half" truck. The road to Saigon was a blur of rear guard placements of helicopter pads, bunkers, and guards. The ride into Saigon was almost surreal. A dozen or so guys riding in the uncovered back of a truck along the road between Bien Hoa and Saigon. As we crossed the river, I took note of the guard shacks and armed guards protecting the bridge. As we drove through town,

I noticed the worn out houses and dirty streets. People were everywhere: on the door stoops, on short stools on the sidewalks; on motorcycles, some with three or four people. We barreled through town without slowing down. We were being transported the few kilometers (I was now in a metric world) to Saigon and MACV Headquarters. After that hectic ride, we were dropped off at 509th headquarters. We would be billeted there for orientation before we would continue on to our final destination. Looking back "final destination" should have sounded ominous, but I was still in the moment. We waited ... and waited for billeting (housing) orders. Once we were assigned to a camp, our duffle bags were dropped off. Then it was a ride to MACV for the first day of orientation. After a short orientation to Viet Nam, it was back to Davis Station, which was the headquarters for the 509th Radio Research Group and the associated field stations throughout the country. That name explained why the recruiter could truthfully say ASA cannot be in a War Zone. Indeed, we were "Radio Research". We weren't "combatants" nor "spies". We were doing "research"! This gave me a brief lesson in the way governments and people rename difficult ventures. Davis Station was a small settlement of "hootches" set next to the flight line of Tan Son Nhật Airport. A busy airport with passenger jets and fighter jets sharing its runways.

As 1972 began I was thoroughly and undeniably in the heat of Viet Nam without a clue about what my future, if I would have one, would be. The GI culture in a war zone is a strange one. A person meets and makes buddies from all walks of American life. The rich, the poor, the education, illiterate were mixed together and trained in the same way. My world took a dramatic turn that became the cornerstone of my road to Viet Nam.

First came the waiting outside the headquarters office for the assignment to temporary quarters while we completed in-country orientation. Each of us had our own story to tell, but few were talking much. Most of us believed we were in dire straits and didn't know what to expect. Orientation took a few days before we would report to our assigned field stations. After Orientation I was notified that my orders had been changed. Instead I was reassigned to headquarters. At first I was given duties as a clerk in the Transit Office (TO) where incoming and outgoing GIs were processed. I settled in with Chief Warrant Officer Detwiller in charge. His Vietnamese girlfriend, Van, visited the office daily and became a part of our daily contact with Vietnamese! While I was at the Transit Office processing the outgoing photographer of the Unit, I began a conversation with him about the photography and how I had learned the skill during my time in El Paso. He looked at some of my photos and negatives from Texas then took that conversation to the Commander and recommended I be his replacement at headquarters! Since the draw down had begun, the 509th had to cut the position I was originally assigned (Phu Bai) due to no need for more translator/interpreters. Since I was qualified both in language and photography, and since headquarters had lost their position for a photographer, and I was already in country, the commander took their outgoing photographer's advice and I was suddenly out of the office and into the Graphics lab with cameras, a dark room and two rooms with equipment to copy captured documents, process film, print photos, and prepare presentations for command meetings. I would later be promoted to lead to supervise two graphic artists. We would prepare graphics of troop movements, translate captured documents submitted by Field Operatives and cover Unit Events, which would later include the closing of many fire stations. The war was turning into a cool job for me. I was beginning to realize this part of my life could mean something for a future. By not trying to get out of a situation, it turned into a bonus for me in the years ahead. "Things will work out" was in play, again.

Back in High School I was envious of my buddy, Tom Catlett, because he was the photographer for our Yearbook and the Journalism Class. I enrolled in the class only to be taken out because of a one quarter credit of PE (physical exercise) that was needed for graduation. Me and others who knew me that was wrong. But rules are rules and I put that idea aside. Now, a soldier in a combat zone, I was not just a correspondent, but also a photographer and graphic artist! When I was put in charge I got my first taste of management as well. Looking back, I am amazed at the mass of "gifts" the Army had given me. First the room and board, followed by working knowledge of another language, and finally those skills in writing, photography, and supervision.

Life was beginning to look rosy in those early days in Viet Nam. I met up with a girl from Can Tho, in the far southern end of the country, who moved in with me in an apartment near the airport. By then all my needs and wants were met. I had begun to enjoy being in Viet Nam despite the war that was going on around me. During the weeks and months, I was able to travel throughout the country to photograph closing of Radio Research bases, ceremonies, and, along the way, the sights of Vietnam and her people.

There were a few recon trips and some freebie rides with pilots who were willing to take me around the area for a copy of the pictures with them and their machine. While in town, I was also taking my time visiting and photographing the orphanage the 509th sponsored. On laundry days I would jump in the back of truck and take pictures along the way. And, finally, the afternoons and nights in Saigon were filled with typical antics of soldiers in the rear having good times. After my shift ended I was quick to head to the collection of "Ba muoi ba" stands just outside our camp gate. "Ba muoi ba" and a "banh mi" were my dinner while I chatted up the ladies who stood behind the counter and flirted with whomever would come by. The country, the people, the environment that was Viet Nam was being planted in my soul. I didn't know how deep that would be until decades later, but I was enjoying being there. In February, 1972 while making rounds of the 33 stands, I met one girl who pointed me out among the others. She literally pointed at me. Specifically, she pointed to my last name that was on my uniform- "Johnston". She said it was the name of her former boyfriend who had returned to the US a year or two earlier. Conversations began, liaisons were made, and, eventually, we moved in together. When we met she was living with an Air Force guy who happened to be attached to our group. She described him as a violent drunk when he was in town. She was ready to leave him. One night, after I had secured apartment on my own, she came knocking on my door while a hop-tac waited outside with her booty from his apartment. For the rest of my tour we lived on Pham Hong Thai Street near a swimming pool somewhere in Saigon.

As my year of service was drawing to a close I realized that I liked being in Saigon. I didn't realize that there was a significant draw down of troops while Nixon was President. But I did request and was granted an extension on my tour. I knew that being in Viet Nam was a good thing for me. Another year would be a great way to learn more about this fabulous country that had been torn apart for almost ten years. That, too, would be a sign in later years that my life was being moved in a direction that I could never have imagined for myself. When November rolled around, my extension approved, I took the 30-day leave granted for those who took an extension and visited my family and friends back in Oklahoma.

When I returned near the end of 1972 I was ready to settle into Vietnam more securely. During my absence, the graphics lab was defunded and I was reassigned to the mailroom for headquarters. "Helping" with clearing out the lab, I confiscated and moved some darkroom equipment and a few cameras into the mailroom. Since I had control of the big room for the post I managed to set up a small darkroom and studio for afterhours activity. My memories being recorded would continue to the very end of my time there. That time was much earlier than I anticipated. In January 1973 the Paris Peace Talks were drawing to a close. On the 27th of January they were signed. Troop withdrawal would be concluded by the end of March. As for the Radio Research group, it was time to clear out. That meant all the hi-tech interception equipment would be shipped or destroyed beyond salvage to insure it did not fall into enemy hands and, eventually, end up in Russian tech labs. After all that was done, Davis Station was cleared of material that could not, would not be shipped back to the States. For those of us left, we were given carte blanche to pack our belongings that the Army would ship to wherever we chose. I packed up the little darkroom I had outfitted along with my own personal cameras and prepared to leave. The girl I had been living with since February 1972 said goodbye, I stepped out of the hop-tac and walked through the Tan Son Nhat gate for the last time. I didn't turn around, but a tear was clouding my eye as I made that walk. My hope of staying in Viet Nam began to fade. Would I be back? Only time would tell.

There is never a way to look into the future and discover what your actions and attitudes will be until the days come and go. It's the looking back on those days that reality sets in. In those days of freedom as an individual, under the supervision and direction of the US Army, I realize that I was being prepared for something that would become much greater than I could have imagined. Connecting those dots 45 years later have created a mosaic that paints a picture of God's hand in my life without me knowing it.

Chapter 3 - Back from the War!

The soul is dyed the color of its thoughts. Think only on those things that are in line with your principles and can bear the light of day. The content of your character is your choice. Day by day, what you do is who you become. Your integrity is your destiny — it is the light that guides your way. - Heraclitus

A Whole New World...again

They say war changes people. I have to agree. Civilians, families, and soldiers are affected by the tragedy that wars bring. What is seen, what is felt, what is experienced, that only war can display, are not for human consumption. But conflict and danger can also bring compassion and understanding to someone who is sensitive to the needs of others and the challenge of giving from one's self to help others. It seems that was the reasoning the American government was involved in Viet Nam. It was also a turnaround for me to see what people living in the midst of war cope with when battles are being fought among and around them. What follows tells what the affect will have on an individual.

On my return to Saigon from a 30-day leave I heard President Nixon and Secretary of State Kissinger had reached an agreement with Viet Nam to withdraw American combat troops from Viet Nam. On March 7, 1973 my time and duty ended on the tarmac at Tan Son Nhut Airbase. As I ascended that walkway, I believed I would never see the likes of Viet Nam again. But I wasn't ready to give up on returning to the country I had come to appreciate. Within hours I was back on US soil and bunked in a large dormitory of GIs who had orders to fly out of Oakland to their new duty stations.

Morning reveille meant nothing to me. When someone came around to wake me, I told them "f*ck off". I had arrived late the night before and was getting out of the Army. When I told him I had just come back from 'Nam, he quietly left without comment.

Processing was short. My Honorable Discharge was a piece of paper and a folder containing the formal certificate that I had served. I boarded the jet for Oklahoma in my required khaki uniform as my last act as a soldier in the United States Armed Forces. The Army Security Agency (ASA) would become a part of my memory but my enlistment would be a secret not told for 40 years. Though I had enlisted for four years (to avoid assignment in Viet Nam!) an early out was granted because the year and a half I had left in the four years was not enough time to retrain me and re-assign somewhere. It was much cheaper to just send me home.

Army life wasn't so bad. All the things anyone needed were met, income, food, housing, medical, clothing. But the one thing that was too difficult for me to handle was military conformity. Being what others expect me to be would become the greatest obstacle I would have in fitting in anywhere. Another lesson learned about myself that distinctly applies to reaching the end of my Road to Viet Nam.

When I landed in Oklahoma City Airport, the khakis were quickly changed into civilian clothes. I was no longer a GI and, thus, no longer needed to dress like one. Walking through the airport to meet whomever would be there to greet me would not see a soldier. Instead they would see a son, brother, grandson, or friend returning. If only a return to civilian life would have been so easy. I had dropped out of University over two years earlier. I had a job that was a good stepping-stone to a position with State Government. My enlistment pushed that stepping-stone away. My marriage was annulled because of the enlistment as well. Enlisting in the Army and going to Viet Nam more or less cut all ties to civilian life for those two and a half years. Getting back into the swing of things was going to be challenging.

Moving in with the family wasn't going to work out. I applied for State unemployment. With military training as a Vietnamese (Northern dialect) Translator/Interpreter as my resume, there wasn't much call in 1973 for jobs in that field. I did contact the Federal State Department and other agencies hoping for a civilian position that would take me back to Viet Nam, but nothing was forthcoming. Perhaps my work as a Combat Photographer would help with applications to National Geographic or Rockwell Aviation, and other businesses where a photographer might be hired. I finally got a job working for the United States Geological Survey, Water Resources Division, Surface Water Section as a Hydrologic Technician. I had no idea what that would be. But, because I was a Veteran, one of the only good things civilian life offered, I got preference over other applicants. The pay was good so I took it. Maybe the road to Viet Nam was truly closed. Getting back into some kind of social life would also be a challenge. First, I began looking up former girlfriends. Connie, Jan, Jean, even Linda. Linda, especially. Since Viet Nam was now behind me, I hoped we could start all over again. But she had already gone her own way. My lost cause joined the pile of former life remnants. But then, I was still writing to my Vietnamese girlfriend, Peanuts, back in Saigon. Of course, emails and internet were not available yet. Letters were those pieces of paper that on which we would scribble or type words. We then had to go to the post office to get the proper amount of postage to send them half-way around the world. Each letter took about two to three weeks to send and a reply to be returned! As I got settled into my new job, the thought came to me that maybe I should ask her to come be with me in the USA. I think my invitation was something like "Would you come to America to cook rice for me?". Yeah, I know, stupid! But she was wise enough to say "No, not unless you marry me." Of course, that was what I meant but she, obviously and cautiously wanted to see those words in writing. When I mentioned the idea to my Supervisor, Mr. Willard Mills, he immediately put on his Deacon of First Baptist Church of Oklahoma City hat to counsel me about a war bride. The paperwork took a few months. She arrived in September 1973. In a very strange turn, I was back on the Road to Viet Nam without knowing it.

Once she arrived, one of the first questions I asked her was about her son, Phuong. He was the child born out of wedlock by her boyfriend whose last name was the same as mine. The reason she gave about why she didn't make bringing him with her was that she was afraid to ask that I adopt another man's son as my own. I met her because of him. His last name is the same as mine. Though there was no apparent relationship except a common family name, it became the thread that got me back on that road. When I agreed to get him to the US, it took another nine months to get her six-year-old son to the USA. By July, 1974 we were one of those "Blended Families" that was becoming the new face of the American family.

Now that I had a family to support and protect it was time to begin looking for other Vietnamese who might be living in Oklahoma City. There were very few Vietnamese we could find who had married Americans. Though there were a couple of ladies who were in such marriages, those friendships didn't work out as well as I had hoped for her. When we would go shopping and see someone that might be Vietnamese, my new wife would not engage. I, on the other hand, would make a connection by asking. I believed that knowing someone from your home country helps to ease the challenge of living in a foreign land. Helping her to find other Vietnamese would give her opportunity to step out of the house and engage in conversation with someone of her own language while she was refining her English.

It wasn't until the "fall" of Saigon on April 30, 1975 that the possibility of meeting Vietnamese would begin to grow. April 30, 1949 was her birthday. On her 26th birthday in 1975, while we were celebrating, the evening news was broadcasting the last American helicopter taking off from the roof of a building near the US Embassy, Saigon. The first wave of refugees would soon be arriving on American soil. For me, it was the final nail, I thought, to prevent me from ever thinking about returning. Perhaps I had misread my feelings about returning to Viet Nam. Instead, I wondered, I must have been preparing to help the new refugees that would be streaming on our shores after 1975.

Though the road back seemed to stop, the need for what the Army had taught me suddenly came to the forefront. Cuc helped many incoming refugees and my language skills were re-awakened. By the end of 1976 we had already begun making friends and helping other Vietnamese get resettled in Oklahoma. Secretly, I wondered if there were something special at work that would explain this unusual turn of events.

When our hopes and dreams seem to end, they might actually be either sleeping, or placed on hold while other things take precedence. As I watched the influx of Vietnamese refugees in America grow, I realized this could be what I was thinking about during my efforts to return to Viet Nam as a civilian.

Thinking about the exciting life of the Army and Viet Nam, I had to ask myself why did I want to return? The more refugees I helped and befriended, the more I began to realize that people are the energy that moves me to act. The Vietnamese are friendly, courteous, kind, and caring people. In many ways they are like the best of Americans. In their plight to find safety, they became refugees from what they believed would be the blood bath that was discovered in nearby Cambodia. They knew their association with the foreign powers would be looked upon by the new government would make their future dangerous. To them, escaping their homeland was their best choice. Maybe my road to Viet Nam was not the country itself, but the people who were coming in droves to American shores.

A Spiritual Awakening

During that time of helping refugees, changes in our family began to take place. Her son, Phuong, was regularly visiting three after-school activities that were sponsored by local Christian churches. John Kuhlman, then the pastor of Brookline Baptist Church in Oklahoma City, led Phuong to accept Jesus as his Savior during one of those after-school activities. John visited us to ask our permission to baptize him. Through that connection and Cuc's interest in Christianity, John brought her a Gideon bi-lingual (English and Vietnamese) New Testament published by the American Bible Society.

Later, after many conversations between John and me, she and I were baptized at his church. I had been a Christian since I was 10 years old, but I had never had been baptized. To encourage her and understand the importance of baptism, both of us went under the waters. With her new spiritual journey came a concern for her family. To help with that concern, John brought her a Vietnamese translation of the Bible published by the American Bible Society. I circled the passages known as the "Roman Road" which helps a non-Christian to know the path to eternal life through faith in Jesus as Savior.

With this new interest in a spiritual life, I began to think that my days in El Paso and Saigon were coming together as a mission from God. As unlikely as everything was, I reasoned, that God must have been leading all along the way without me having a clue about his plans. For the next five years our lives were balanced and busy with a variety of works. Professionally, I became a supervisor at the USGS. I also opened a small photo studio (from skills I learned in the Army). I also tried my hand at multi-level marketing as an Amway distributor. During that time, I also took on the role of a landlord with two rental houses and some property in Oklahoma City. Personally, I was learning how to be a better step-father, husband, and home-owner. My road was suddenly getting very cluttered with work and responsibility that was pushing the dream of returning to Viet Nam to live behind me.

Socially, we began to expand our friendships to include many newcomers. My family gatherings in Shawnee were better attended. My co-workers at the USGS were friendships that grew. The spiritual side of my life was my greatest area of growth. For two decades I "rested" as a baby Christian. At 10 years old life as a Christian was about fun activities at Church and Sunday school. Through their efforts, love, and prayers of my grandmothers Ivey and Johnston I steadily grew in "grace and wisdom" but I never really got tied into religion or the church. Reading and understanding the Bible was my part-time quest. It was enough to teach Cuc the basics of being Christian. Eventually, with a family to attend to and the encouragement of Pastor and friend Kuhlman, I became much more involved in the work of Brookline Baptist Church and my own growth as a Christian.

First was as a student in a Sunday School class. That led to me teaching bible classes. Which brought the invitation to direct the Sunday as the Minister of Education. Holding that title, "Minister", encouraged me to get involved with the local Baptist Association of churches to attend their night courses in ministry studies. Independent correspondence courses added to my ministerial education. By 1981, I had committed myself to resigning the USGS and enroll in Southwestern Baptist Theological Seminary in Fort Worth, Texas. I started in the Associate Degree of Religious Education. But I wanted more. So I moved to Dallas Baptist University to get a Bachelor's degree in Pastoral Ministry that allowed me to return to Seminary in the Masters of Divinity degree program. With a religious training and a theology education I was prepared to address the spiritual, emotional, and physical needs of the Vietnamese refugees that were now numbered in the tens of thousands throughout the USA. By the beginning of the 1980s My Road to Viet Nam seemed firmly set before me. Ministry among the Vietnamese in the USA by helping Christian Vietnamese establish churches to reach the growing number of them arriving on our shores.

Finding My Path

Personally, I was learning how to be a better step-father, husband, and home-owner. Socially we began to expand our friendships to include many newcomers. Family gatherings in Shawnee were better attended and my co-workers at the USGS built friendships that were strong. Spiritually was my greatest area of growth. For two decades I "rested" as a baby Christian. At 10 life as a Christian was about fun activities at Church and Sunday school. Through the efforts and prayers of my Grandmothers Ivey and Johnston and their love I steadily grew in "grace and wisdom" but I never really got tied into religion or church. Reading and understanding the Bible was my part time quest. It was enough to teach Cuc the basics of being Christian. Eventually, with a family to attend to and the encouragement of Pastor and friend Kuhlman, I became much more involved in the work of Brookline Baptist Church and my own growth as a Christian. First was as a student in a Sunday School class. That led to me teaching bible classes. Which brought the invitation to direct the Sunday as the Minister of Education. Holding that title, "Minister", encouraged me to get involved with the local Baptist Association of churches to attend their night courses in ministry studies. Soon independent correspondence courses added to my ministerial education. By 1981, I had committed myself to leaving the USGS and enroll in Southwestern Baptist Theological Seminary in Fort Worth, Texas. I started in the Associate Degree of Religious Education. But I wanted more. So I moved to Dallas Baptist University to get a Bachelor's degree in Pastoral Ministry that allowed me to return to Seminary in the Masters of Divinity degree. With a religious education trainings and a theology degree I was prepared to address the spiritual and physical needs of the Vietnamese refugees that were now numbered in the tens of thousands throughout the USA.

By the beginning of the 1980s my Road to Viet Nam seemed firmly set before me. Mission Minister to the Vietnamese in the USA by helping Christian Vietnamese establish churches to reach the growing number of them arriving on our shores.

Return to Civilian Life

By the end of 1975 I found myself visiting newly arrived families and hearing first hand their escape from the hands of communism. Many had anticipated a blood bath similar to the "killing fields" of Cambodia just months before. But most seemed to be looking for a safe haven to renew their life without the supposed restriction and incarceration expected in the aftermath. In that environment I found my experience and language skills were suddenly needed again. I volunteered to the call.

Over the next few years as the number of refugees grew and settled into Oklahoma City, I found myself recalling the people I had met and got to know while living in Saigon. Meeting the refugee families and helping them navigate the array of assistance that had become available to them became a resurrection and maybe a reconciliation of serving as a soldier during the "American War" (as the conflict is called in Viet Nam these days). Those 47 weeks of Vietnamese language training that I had never officially used during my 16 months in country were now coming to bear in doctor's offices, hospital wards, and social services. I also began to make new friends that my Vietnamese wife could get to know.

Suddenly, without realizing what was happening, I look back and understand I was still on the road to Viet Nam. It's more than interesting to look back on those days and remember the events that followed to understand that there seemed to be a plan in the making that would continue to develop my skills and compassion for a country where American men and women fought and died and abandoned with the capitulation to the Communist North. I was back on my road to Viet Nam without doing or planning anything at all.

In 1968 I thought it would be great to major in Chemical Engineering. So I enrolled at Oklahoma State University to begin that career! After all, it was 1968 and maybe I could design a new drug! But after a year I realized I wasn't cut out for the details and connections that chemistry required. It was then that the Army put me on a new career path for four years. While taking the year of language training at Ft. Bliss, I enrolled in two computer language classes (FORTRAN and COBOL). Little did I know that those business and science languages would be so 70s and out of use in the next decade!

Ending my Vietnamese language training, I headed to Viet Nam with no expectations. I did my year there, requested a six-month extension. If I could have stayed that full six months, I probably would have asked for another tour. Despite my training, I was assigned to be Graphics Lab NCOIC. With my new MOS of Combat Photographer I would be able to travel the land and meet the people while recording my unit's activities, which ended up being Base closing ceremonies. The American intervention in Viet Nam was ending. Though I felt like I was finally on a track that would bring fulfillment in a career as a translator/interpreter or photographer, it was not going to be in Viet Nam.

1973 my honorable discharge meant I would get hiring preferences in most any government job. But the withdrawal of US combat troops, I was left hanging for any jobs relating to Vietnamese. But there was the photographer career that was open. Rockwell Aircraft, National Geographic, and a host of lesser companies were not hiring! It was the USGS that hired me as a Hydrologic Technician, a new career path. Only 23 years old and I had switched careers five times. Then, I married my girlfriend from the last days of my VN tour to the States on October 5 of that year. Things slowed down after that.

In July 1976 I sponsored her six-year-old son to join us in the USA. Now we were a family. Maybe my career was set as that Hydrologic Technician. I settle down into what looked like a lifetime as a civil servant, wading the rivers and streams of Oklahoma and taking culture growths for water quality. Over the 10 years working at the USGS, I advanced to supervisor, bought some property, and lived in a spacious two-story house in a nice section of Oklahoma City. I even signed up as an Amway distributor (though I wasn't very good at it).

But I couldn't forsake what I learned as a photographer. My interest in the skill started back in high school when my buddy, Tom Catlett, who was yearbook photographer, was always getting me out of class to "help him" with an assignment. So, I opened a small in-home studio and rigged a small darkroom to make some extra income and improve my skills. Life seemed fairly comfortable. Wife, stepson, a nice house, some rental income, a dab of income from Amway, and some fun and profit with photos. Thoughts of returning to Viet Nam were slowly fading. That is until 1977.

In 1975, the government of South Viet Nam collapsed. The country borders closed while the new, communist government held the reins of power. When April 30 arrived thousands of Vietnamese living in the south and central regions of Viet Nam fled their homeland in fear of severe retributions for collaborating with Western countries. A lion's share of the refugees was taken in by the US Government. They were resettled across the USA. Some landed in Oklahoma. After visiting a few of the newly resettled families I realized that maybe my language skill would find an outlet.

Chapter 4 - Spiritual misdirection 1981-1988

The Bible story about Jonah tells of a man who tried to run away from God who was sending him to Nineveh. No matter how he tried Jonah could not escape the inevitable. In 1981 I had all but lost the desire to return to Viet Nam. My attention was redirected to a spiritual path focused on religious education within the Christian Church. News from Viet Nam was silent. The "First Wave" of refugees was subsiding. American movie makers were filling the screens with anti-Vietnam stories of rescue and retribution to convince Americans that the war was behind us. I, too, put Viet Nam behind me. I enrolled in Southwestern Baptist Theological Seminary (SWBTS) in Fort Worth, Texas. My major was Religious Education. My goal was to be prepared for a career as an Educational Administrator or Minister of Education (in the vernacular of the church) by earning a degree in Religious Education. I was taking a different path.

In 1981 I was integrally involved with religious education of myself and the congregation of Brookline Baptist Church. I became, first, a teacher and choir member. Soon I was Sunday School Director. I began taking night courses sponsored by the local Association of Baptist Churches. Finally, I was ordained to the Gospel ministry. It seemed I had taken a new road, a professional cleric. Pastor Kuhlman and others at Brookline encouraged me to earn a degree in Religious Education at Seminary.

By the end of 1981 I had resigned my position at the USGS, sold my properties in Oklahoma City, including our home there. We loaded up my old pickup truck, a small U-Haul trailer, and the family car and headed South to Texas. The plan was to live in seminary housing while attending classes full time. When we arrived we were told there were no apartments available on campus. A quick search led us to an apartment a short distance from Travis Avenue Baptist Church (TABC).

TABC was the largest church I had ever been in. The campus and parking lot covered a full city block. Our first visits there were friendly encounters and encouragement to join their congregation. We did. A few weeks later, we were approached by Ruth Boone, a member who was responsible for the Literacy Mission and the Vietnamese Mission that was established a few months earlier. The current pastor of the congregation was also a Seminary student but had no connection with Vietnamese other than leading the mission. Within a few weeks of my arrival he graduated and moved on. I was asked to take his place as the new Pastor. I didn't realize it at the time, but I was being led back onto my road to Viet Nam.

My story differs from Biblical Jonah's story. He resisted his calling to preach God's message to Ninevah. Though I was reticent to be a preacher, I was humbled to accept and appreciated the change in direction for my ministerial life. On August 2, 1982 I preached my first sermon to that small congregation of Vietnamese refugees. Some were Christians and others were there because TABC had helped them resettle in Ft. Worth. I also began teaching English as a Second Language (ESL) at the Literacy Mission that Ruth was also directing. The Mission was using the Laubach Method. "Each One, Teach One" was its motto. The idea was to help a student enough to help another student. The multiplication strategy expanded much like the way I learned from my short time as an Amway Distributor. That provided the foundation of ministry that I would carry with me for the rest of my days in Texas. The Literacy Mission reached out to all non-English speakers in the Ft. Worth area. Through the Tarrant County Literacy Association, we were able to teach adults from Mexico, Korea, Japan, and other counties. Once again, I was being primed for something much greater than I could have imagined. Something that would impact my life 26 years later, when I would move to Thailand. Each of these lessons in life were becoming a part of the journey I was on. I was still on my Road to Viet Nam without realizing it. The road that I believed had been closed was being rebuilt without me being aware of where it would lead. As that first year of ministry began to unfold, I thought that I must have been wrong about returning to Viet Nam. My path seemed obvious that I was ordained to help build a Christian community of Vietnamese helping each other to rebuild the lives they left behind when they escaped their war-torn country.

For the next eight years I threw myself into the ministry to the Vietnamese in America. Through our mission at TABC we helped resettle new arrivals through agencies like the SBRS (Southern Baptist Refugee Services) and World Relief Refugee Services (WRRS). I believe my association with WRRS was not by chance. Their office, located next to the Seminary's campus was headed by John Parsons who was also married to a Vietnamese. As a civilian, he had also given missionary service for a while in Viet Nam. We often met and talked about our parallel lives and experiences with Vietnamese. Working with WRRS and the Southern Baptist Refugee Services drew the attention of my State Baptist Convention. In 1984, the Baptist General Convention of Texas (BGCT) Missions Division approached me for the position of Catalytic Missionary for a statewide approach to the new wave of refugees entering the US. Dallas and Houston metropolitan areas were receiving hundreds of new arrivals. With only a handful of churches able to offer limited help with resettlement, the BGCT expanded their efforts in Church starting into the growing Vietnamese communities. By the end of 1984 I had passed on my role as Pastor to new, young Seminary student, Paul Pham, whose family was among the first wave that came out of Viet Nam in 1975. His father was a Pastor in their hometown of Pleiku and was serving a Vietnamese Church in West Virginia. Paul was the fulfillment of Laubach's "Each One, Teach One" philosophy!

With Paul in the pulpit, I began doing research and building strategies for planting Vietnamese churches in Texas. From as far west as El Paso, East to Marshall, North to Amarillo and South to Polacios, I searched for pockets of Vietnamese communities, sought out established churches who were willing to sponsor a Vietnamese ministry, and train workers in outreach methodologies to support their efforts. As the number of Bible Ministries grew and as some evolved into Vietnamese churches, I began training Vietnamese leadership in Church organization. The lack of Vietnamese bible study material launched a widening scope in my new life as a homeland missionary.

The national organization of Southern Baptists Convention (SBC) had begun to notice the growing impact Texas was having on the ethnic communities. They invited me to work with them on feasibility studies in various cities across America. They also enlisted me to write a set of bible study books for the growing number of Vietnamese ministries. By 1986 I was appointed as a Missionary Associate with the SBC Home Mission Board. My opportunities opened doors across the USA. My work with the TABC Church continued. I often helped local families as translator and advocate with City and County organizations as well as greeting arriving family reunifications at the airport. In Texas my work with the BGCT expanded to conducting leadership workshops and cooperative meetings with other Baptists entities. Contacts through the national network also led to assisting the network of all denominations of Vietnamese church leaders to begin a new translation of the Bible. The existing translation was outdated and filled with Roman Catholic terminology that differed from the evangelical theologies. That band of men and women brought together Vietnamese scholars and ministers who were using the Greek and Hebrew scripts for a clearer and more accurate translation from the original languages.

As 1987 came around it was clear and I was confident about my calling. My Army Language Training, my marriage to a Vietnamese woman, my involvement with Vietnamese communities throughout the US, and the satisfaction that I was where God wanted me to serve him were all signs that I had reached my destination. In the middle of 1987, I attended a missions conference on the West Coast on the Golden Gate Baptist Seminary campus which was located across the bay over Golden Gate Bridge of San Francisco. The ministry opportunities took another major turn in my life. Coming back to Texas, I couldn't get San Francisco out of my mind. I remembered Tony Bennett's famous song "I Left My Heart in San Francisco". For the next year I prayed and sought understanding of whether I was truly in love with San Francisco or was God redirecting my path. At the same time two positions opened in San Francisco: Director of Missions for the Southern Baptist Churches and Director of Refugee Services for World Relief. I applied and interviewed for both. I was on the Road again!

Taking a left turn - 1988-1996

Moving to San Francisco never crossed my mind until that Missions Conference. The "Left Coast" was a mystery that I wasn't prone to investigate. The only time I had been to the West Coast was a vacation in 1976 to visit my aunts and their families in a small town about 40 miles east of San Francisco. When the two positions opened, I felt compelled to respond. If neither came through that would be enough to let me know I should continue to serve in Texas.

In those weeks before sending my resume West, a fellow Catalytic Missionary was getting ready to take his second retirement. He and his wife had served in China for 25 years. He was selected to do a similar job as mine but among the Chinese populations of Texas. His few years in Texas would be the time he needed to wait for a full retirement. It was 1988 and I was offered to add his position with the Chinese Churches to my responsibilities to the Vietnamese works. Over the seven years working with Vietnamese I was a part in helping the 15 small Vietnamese groups grow to 47 works. Two of the churches in Texas had purchased their own buildings to develop ministries of their own. "Each one, teach one" was working! It's principles remained with me throughout my years of teaching. Later in 1988, I drove my little Ford Fiesta from Texas to California over two days and nights. Reaching highway 1 leading into San Francisco a record breaking storm hit as I was driving up the coast. Winds recorded as high as 100 mph were pounding the coast. My little Fiesta held tight to the coastal highway as I neared my destination. An omen? I chose to take it a sign that I must weather such storms in life if I am to be strengthened for the work ahead. Once more, a life's event gave me a lesson that I could hold onto later.

I have to give credit of that philosophy to my preaching professor, Joel Gregory, at SWBTS. His instructions to the class taught me some important principles in preaching as well as public speaking. One being the use of everyday events to illustrate biblical principles. Dr. Gregory's preaching at Gambrel Baptist Church where he was Pastor and, later, when he was speaker at the regular service at Dallas Baptist University, I heard him preach the same sermon but spoken differently. He began that sermon in the same way - "There is a four letter word that you almost never hear from Baptists". Certainly many words came to mind. But the four points of his sermon were illuminated as R I S K! I was not the kind of Baptist that was afraid to utter and act on that word. Driving half way across the country and all of those 1,400 miles I wondered if the risk I was taking was truly what I thought God was doing in my life. First, I met with Dr. Francis DuBose. I had read one of his books while in Seminary. He was a consummate and noted authority on Urban Missions. Sitting across from him I felt comfortable as anyone should expect from someone who has made missionary life his life's work. He was honest with me during the interview. Another Seminary graduate of Golden Gate Baptist Seminary, Karl Ortis, had also interviewed for the position. Both of us were "contenders". The other position was for Director of the Bay Area World Relief Refugee Services. The outgoing director had left to work in China. Sitting with Regional

Director Ron Curtain, I felt an unusual excitement about giving first hand assistance to resettling refugees from around the world. Each positions seemed certain and clear that I would be ready and able to assume either role. When I returned to Ft. Worth, the word came from World Relief that I had been chosen to fill the position. Word also came that Karl had been chosen for the Missions Director. My resignation from the USGS was effective November 30, 1988. Our house was sold by mid-December. We were packed and heading West by December 28, 1988. Almost a duplicate of our move to Fort Worth, Texas in December 26, 1981. Driving into San Francisco left me with a feeling that I was, somehow, coming home. I'd only been there twice, once in 1976 on a vacation to visit family in nearby Antioch and Brentwood. The other was the Missions Conference at Golden Gate Seminary in 1986. But I have often taken such perceptions as a sign that I've made the right decision. The storm that hit as I was coming into the interview visit along with a few other instances I have considered signs that the years I spent in San Francisco were more of a test for whether I could cope with living overseas. Over the time spent in California I was in contact with many people from many different countries, both generational citizens and immigrants.

My work experience was beginning to tell me something about myself. But that realization would have to wait. There were storms ahead that would confirm my suspicions. My work at World Relief lasted a year. In that time, I computerized the process of resettlement that allowed staff to give more time to helping the refugees. I opened two field offices, one in San Jose to have a local contact with the refugees who were being reunited with their families from an earlier migration and the other in West Sacramento where many Hmong were already settling and a contact point for the new flood of Soviet refugees. In addition to the field offices, I opened a liaison with the Central Valley office in Lodi to accommodate the Hmong/Laotian refugees in Sacramento. It was my disappointment with the leadership of the Region, e.g. Mr. Curtin, that precipitated my firing. But, as has been said by many, when one door closes, another opens.

The First Baptist Church, San Francisco was the church we joined on our arrival to San Francisco. Within walking distance from our apartment it was both convenient, accurately placed in the center of the City, and we were readily welcomed and received, as we were at Travis Avenue Church back in

Ft. Worth. In addition to First Baptist and my association with the Baptist Association as Refugee Resettlement director, Rev. Karl Ortis invited me to accept the role of Missions Minister for the local Baptist Association. Dr. Jim Higgs, Pastor of First Baptist, at the same time offered me a part time job as Church Secretary. Between the two organizations I was able to continue my calling to serve in the name of the Lord. Both works offered challenging but fruitful work.

Another confirmation that convinced me that I had made the right choice to move West. In October, 1989 San Francisco was shaken by the Loma Prieta Earthquake. I had just gotten to our apartment when I felt the building shaking, pictures began falling off the walls, things on the shelves were falling. For 15 seconds, our world literally shook. When it was over, we were ok. The building was intact. From our sixth floor viewpoint we surveyed the after effects. Emergency services were activated. The park across the street from our apartment building was used as an emergency field for helicopters and medical teams. Electricity was out. No phone service for a while. We were isolated for a few hours. We walked down the six flights of stairs to walk around the neighborhood. It seemed reasonable to be outside since we didn't know if aftershocks would endanger our building or not. A local ice cream store was open and offering free ice cream since it would be melting if the electricity wasn't restored soon. Over the next few days I walked around the city to see what other damage was inflicted by the quake. The most dramatic effect the Quake had on our lives arrived nine months later with the birth of our son, Nathanael Tran-Nguyen Johnston. Out of the rubble and carnage of the Quake came new life. My son was born. The hope of the 17 years of marriage and questions of whether we would ever have the joy of a child that was mine ended. Or so we thought. I was not longer just a step-father. I was and ever would be a father. Everything seemed right. From July 24, 1990 (Nate's birthday) my life would be devoted to being a father. Work would, for the first time, become secondary to my life.

In 1992 my wife made her first visit to her family in Viet Nam. When she left them in 1973 to come to America to be my wife, she left her son behind. In 1974, I was able to get him to America to join us. In 1975, the liberation of the South closed the doors to Viet Nam for 10 years. When she finally was able to get in touch with her family she began sending money to help them survive the rigors of the new government of Viet Nam. From my association with World Relief and the Vietnamese churches in the Bay Area, the contacts we had with Vietnamese refugees gave us a second look at what was going on in her homeland in those years.

In 1985, the country finally opened up a bit for visitors to come and go with relative ease. When she finally decided to visit in 1992, Nate was only two years old. I decided it would not be wise for him to go with her at such a young age. She returned for a couple of months to renew her ties with family while I took the role of "single parent" while she was away. It was the most exciting time of life. Taking care of my son was the perfect bonding at that young age. Thanks to Ann Higgs, a friend and church member, who took care of Nate during my days at work. I was free of worries about him, and enjoyed the evenings with him thoroughly. When she returned to Viet Nam again in 1995, Nate, now five years old, was able to go with her. It was the loneliest time I had ever felt. I prepared a video recording that I sent with a friend who was also going to Viet Nam. As I poured my heart out as if I were talking to Nate I realized how much he meant to me. During that period, though I didn't realize it at that time, I was also voicing my longing to be back in Viet Nam. It would take another five years before I could construct my thoughts of returning.

During those first years in San Francisco, the work with the Church and Association flourished. I was able to get an abandoned building funded to be restored and converted to a community outreach center. Reaching out to the Red Cross Disaster Services I was trained and enrolled a number of churches in their training. I continued to keep in contact with the Vietnamese Community by participating in the organization of the annual Convention of Evangelical Vietnamese Churches. I often accepted invitations to teach, preach, and train at churches in San Francisco. For a brief term I was even a ministry reflection group facilitator at Golden Gate Seminary. Like Texas, work in San Francisco was fruitful as long as I stayed in touch with the communities, their people and their activities. It was only when I questioned the motives and methods of leadership that I would garner disfavor among leaders. In 1996 another storm struck. As I became more involved in the ministry and administration of First Baptist Church I was promoted to Office manager, then Administrative Pastor. Managing the four buildings and grounds on the corner of Octavia and Waller Streets along with reaching out to the community by offering limited facilities to community groups to meet, conflicts with other leaders in the Church were beginning to pop up. Working with Church committees and community groups was a delicate balance of administration and civic participation. In 1991, I decided to resign from the Association Missions Minister work and focus entirely on efforts at First Baptist. For a short time, I substitute taught as needed at the Church's International School. When the Principal left, I stood in that position for a few months before a new principal was hired. With all the work that I was doing I noticed a marked division being aggravated by the Pastor's absence during his six-month sabbatical in an eastern university. When he returned, changes were made that seemed to ignore the honored seniors and singles of the church. The new directions and marketing the Pastor and his family members instituted were bringing division into the church. When I spoke about it to some members, I was quickly fired. No cause was given, but I realized it was the same problem I faced with the World Relief position. I voiced my opposition to leadership and was dismissed. Lesson learned. My days of ministry and working within church boundaries was weakening. My disappointment with leadership in churches left me with questions that I could not answer. For a short time, I led a youth group at San Mateo Chinese Church. But my heart was not in it.

At the end of 1996, I left working with any church and took a part time job with the City and County of San Francisco. For two or three hours in the mornings, I worked in the Main Frame Computer Center of the County separating daily computer printouts and reports for the various departments throughout the City.

A new road was ahead. A new career was on the horizon. A new direction was born out of the conflict and confusion of what church work can be. It was my son who became the center of my world. He became the only source of inspiration and hope for my future. Too much confusion between people and ministry had taken its toll on me. I turned my attention away from ministry and toward the world for income. My spiritual life turned inward as I worked more as a Christian father to my son. The road ahead was dark but I was willing to take the risk to move ahead along the new route.

Chapter 5 - Bi-Vocational - 1996-2000

One of the great changes in America came in the 1960 decade. By the end of the decade wives were beginning to work outside the home. Husbands would often have two jobs or work extended hours to "make ends meet". The cost of living in the USA was steadily increasing but the American home had become a household of materialism. Families were being torn apart by separate social activities for babies, children, teens, younger and older adults. Wives and Husbands were divided with their own forms of entertainment. Spiritually I could see that the costs associated with the changes was not inflation. Families were drifting apart. Caught up in that world was an easy road with two incomes.

In Mid-July 1996 I was one of the unemployed. The last time I had been without a job was in 1973 when I returned home from my tour in Viet Nam. For a couple of months, I took life easy while making a few job interviews. Finding a job back then was fairly easy, especially for a Veteran. In 1991 I had been working 50-60 hours a week as the "Church Secretary", though many of the congregation saw me as an associate pastor responsible for the management and upkeep of our 50,000 square feet of facilities as well as a standby counselor. Through the building and grounds committee I carried out their decisions on a daily basis. I was also teaching a bible study on Sunday mornings, leading an occasional Wednesday night prayer service, and often attending or giving oversight to the many meetings that would visit our facilities. On July 7th, 1996 I was given 15 minutes to clear my desk, turn in my church keys to the resident missionary and vacate the offices. Dumbfounded would aptly describe my feelings at that time.

But I had to get on with my life. I had a family, Nate was still enrolled in First Baptist's International School, and there were financial obligations I had to pay. Within a few weeks two friends helped make my transition from full time ministry to bi-vocational work. Sharon Flack was Director of the local Child Evangelism Fellowship. My wife was her secretary. She told me about a Chinese church in San Mateo who was looking for a Youth Minister. I interviewed with them and began a short term effort to drive the 30 miles south for two evenings a week to give spiritual leadership and counseling to their teenagers.

Thanks went to many church members at First Baptist who would slip me money to help with expenses. Calvin Chow, one of those church members, helped me secure a job with the San Francisco Department of Health. It was only a two hour a day job but the pay was good and allowed me time to think on what had happened that caused the immediate dismissal from the job I had grown into over the six years at FBC. Getting up at 4 a.m. every day to catch the Mission Street bus to the downtown Main Frame operations center, I would gather daily printouts for the Health Department's various facilities scattered around town. After my two hours of separating reports, I had time to sit with a cup of coffee and pen in hand to sort through the state I was in.

For the next five months I would hobble through my few hours of work during the week to earn just enough to meet the bare minimum of household expenses. I felt my life of Christian ministry was beginning to wane. In 1997, I was offered some part time consultant work at the Department of Human Resources (DHR), another department of San Francisco government. It was contract negotiation time of year and they were looking for someone to help them with the typing of 54 labor contracts that were being negotiated by the Employee Relations Division of DHR. That godsend quickly turned into an opportunity for full time work when I showed them what I could do to improve their support staff's computer skills as well as implement some database tools to help manage the many labor contracts the DHR were negotiating. For the next seven years I went from a part time typing assistant to personnel analyst, to database manager, systems analyst, programmer, and, finally, Job Exam Analyst. Through those many jobs within the department, I found a great consolation and enjoyment working with some incredible people. Ministry slowly fell into my background.

The "bi-vocational" part of my life didn't stop with the Youth work in San Mateo. After a few weeks the drive south was costing more in time and gas than I was receiving in pay. Someone had told me about a small church just across Crocker Amazon Park in Visitacion Valley on the outskirts of San Francisco. Just a five-minute walk from our house, I accepted the part time position as their Pastor. During that time, I also accepted invitations to preach in small churches whose pastors were on vacation or were pastor-less. One of those congregations was a small Methodist group in the Sunset District of San Francisco. In 2000 they invited me invited me as their pastor to help them start a home church in the neighborhood.

Suddenly, or so it seems, I was serving two congregations while giving more hours to working at the City job. My days and hours were slowly being filled with enough work to allow me to catch up with the debts I had accumulated during the slow time after getting fired from FBC. 15 hours at Valley Baptist Church, five hours with the Home Church, and 40 hours at the DHR, gave me income of over 100,000$ a year, more than I had ever made in my life. But to put that income in perspective I read a humorous quip about how to know if a person is poor in San Francisco. One standard read, "You know you are poor in San Francisco is you are only making 100,000$ a year". I didn't give much thought to the joke, but I did know that 8,500$ a month didn't seem to go very far. I managed it as best I could. Nate was in a private school, we were able to take some nice trips throughout the year, and our house had enough stuff to keep us occupied during the week.

Life was settled or so I thought. In 2000 (remember Y2K scares?) 27 years after I left Viet Nam as a soldier, I made plans to join my wife and Nate in Ho Chi Minh City (formerly Saigon). My wife had returned for two-three months every other year since that her first 1992 visit. Again in 1995, 1997, 1998, and finally, in 2000, I decided I wanted to join her. It was then, the seed took root. I considered the possibility of retiring there. Returning to Viet Nam was filled with anxiety and anticipation. I had no idea what to expect. The country had been under Communism for 25 years. What would that mean for me as a former soldier in their war for Independence? Rumors came to me about messages being handed off secretly and government "watchers" of foreign visitors? Just like the day in 1971 when I first set foot on Vietnamese soil, I was walking the same tarmac of Tan Son Nhat Airport. I had two weeks to discover Viet Nam again.

Walking from the airplane to the terminal I remembered the heat when I de-planed in 1971 wearing newly issued jungle fatigues. Then it was a small building with tin roof. Now it was bigger and air conditioned. The walk to the terminal was still hot, but once inside, I could appreciate the change. The jungle fatigues were replaced by my pressed cotton shirt with tie and slacks. I looked more like a business man than a guy on vacation. To prepare me for immigration, my wife suggested I put a $5 bill in my passport when I approached the immigration officer. I chose not to do that. My walk up to the officer was friendly and quick. I was through immigration in what seemed like record time. A bit bewildered I collected my 70 kilograms of goods from the US and walked through the terminal to the waiting crowd outside. A chain link fence separated the waiting families. Walking slowly, I desperately searched for the one face I knew best, Nate's. The walk seemed long, but eventually, there he was, perched on the shoulders of his uncle. I couldn't contain my excitement. I was back in Viet Nam and my son was there to greet me. He was only 10 years old but it seemed like I hadn't seen him for ages. Time certainly did make my heart grow fonder for the love of my son. A van full of family was there to greet me. As we loaded up in the van I took a survey of Tan Son Nhat. I didn't remember much from the 27 years behind me. Instead I was more interested in hearing Nate's voice and listening to my wife's update on the family. In the interim I also tried to hear in-laws and understand with my limited recollection of the language. My days of Fort Worth and the Vietnamese language I had maintained then had been lost in the years of living in San Francisco. Now I felt I needed to return to that skill and get up to speed.

Being back was the prelude to getting back on the Road I thought I would never tread again. But being back in old Saigon was familiar and interesting more than I ever imagined. One day, on a visit into District 1 a taxi driver asked if I wanted a ride. When I answered in Vietnamese "không phai" ("no need") he asked me, in English, where I had learned Vietnamese. That began a conversation that lasted a good while. He had a lot of questions and comments like two old Army buddies might have shared from the 27 years that separated us. But the trip back was not limited to Ho Chi Minh City. The three of us made a trip to Nha Trang and Da Lat. It didn't take long before I was convinced I wouldn't mind staying longer. But two weeks was all I had requested from work. When I returned, I was sold. I would be back. That wouldn't be until 2004. In those four years I would pay for the house I bought from my sister-in-law and her husband. I also considered what it would take and what I might do if we were to move to Viet Nam. The visit to Nha Trang was more of a vacation trip to the sea side town. A trip to the white sandy beaches, crystal clear waters, and meals that were fresh and tasty made the visit engaging but not enough to change from visit to residence. It was Da Lat that set the first stake.

This sleepy little mountain town was the first step to enjoy. The 6500-meter elevation was cooler. The mountain sides filled with tea and coffee plantations caught my first attention. Arriving late in the afternoon I saw many large villas that, later I discovered, were abandoned French Villas. Further inquiries led me to discover they could be bought for around 40,000$ US dollars. The hook was set. I began constructing a plan that could would lead me to this final place for me. I was on My Road to Viet Nam one more time.

Chapter 6 - On the Road Again - 2004

2004 was a transitional year. 2002 was intended to be my second trip back to Viet Nam but finances and work would prevent my adventure to continue. With wife and son gone for the summer I was busy with thinking about the trip from 2000. The large villas in Da Lat kept coming to mind. $40,000 for those large multi-story buildings left me with visions of some kind of business that I could enlist her family to work. An institute? A bed and breakfast? It was an adventure to pursue. Coming up with the $40,000 wasn't so much of a problem. But the fact that in those days, foreigners could not own residences or property in Viet Nam. But the idea of living there had already broken ground.

Reviewing my finances over that summer of 2002 was enlightening. If I were to take an early vested retirement from the city job, we would have enough to live there. Though I couldn't imagine living with her family in the already crowded Lac Long Quan house that her mother owned, I could well imagine a place in Nha Trang or, especially, Da Lat. Even though we would have to rent, I could still enjoy the life by the sea or the mountains. Both places offered special appeals. When Nate and his mom came back from their summer in Saigon, she brought a suggestion that changed everything. Her sister's family, living in the house adjacent to her mother's, wanted to move to another district in Ho Chi Minh City. She offered her place to us first. Her asking price was $12,000 (USD). I sent her $1,000 as a down payment while I went about raising another $10,000 to reach our negotiated price of $11,000. It was relatively small, about 1200 square feet, but more than adequate for the two of us. The two of us was the key to moving. Nate was already 14 and comfortable with his schooling at San Francisco Christian School. Taking him away from an American school and pushing him into a Vietnamese school, even if it were an International school, would not be my best decision. I decided that the end of 2008 would be best. He would graduate from high school and be enrolled in an American university. Though California universities would have been nice, his accommodations would be a financial challenge for us on the expected vested retirement from the City. If he could enroll in a university near his step-brother and his family, we could manage an upkeep allowance for Nate to live with him. The plans were beginning to come together. By the end of 2003 I had managed to secure the cost of the house in Saigon and was talking with my step-son about Nate living with his family during his university years. Summer break Nate would stay with us in Viet Nam. Everything seemed to be in order. Plans were made to pay off by the end of 2003 any debts we had. Finally, increase our savings to make the move, put Nate in university, and get him settled.

When I went back to Viet Nam in the summer of 2004 my sister-in-law showed me the paperwork that certified I had paid for the house. Her family moved into the place to make sure it was taken care of. Since her mother's house and the house I had paid for shared a common wall, they cut a doorway connecting the two houses. When Nate and his mom arrived earlier that summer a room in her mom's house was especially prepared for us with a rented air conditioner and a private toilet. Though just a bed and toilet, it was enough to give me a flavor of what living in Viet Nam might be like. Returning from that trip in August 2004, I immediately set about with plans that would help me decide if that transition would be reasonable. First, my language skills would need improving. Secondly, Nate's health and welfare would have to be dealt with. His second leg surgery must be completed. His finances for schooling had to be in the bank, and my vested retirement had to be budgeted to insure it would sustain us and Nate until the other retirement accounts would "kick in". As the plans continued to roll out I was getting excited about the move.

There were two unanswerable issues that I had to deal with emotionally. First was the fact that I, as an American, would be living in the Communist country where I was once their enemy. Would I be segregated or treated differently as a resident? The hatred and fear of Communism became public in the 50s when Senator Joe McCarthy started his witch hunt that began the "Red Scare". Kennedy had come close to nuclear war with Russia in October, 1963 when nuclear missiles were being shipped to Cuba. For decades, living in America, Communism was painted as an "evil empire" as Reagan called it. Second would be a racial issue. I would be a tall, old, white guy living among Vietnamese. Would I be accepted or rejected by the community around District 11 where our house was located? It took a while to resolve those concerns. But my trips to Viet Nam in 2000 and 2004 showed no signs that any resentment or anger was directed toward Americans. In fact, I was met with friendliness and fascination by a younger generation who did not know or care about the wars Viet Nam had fought for their independence. I suspect not many Americans knew anything more about Viet Nam other than the few years we were engaged in their fight for Independence. Discrimination and segregation seemed a distant worry that I put aside for reasons based on being accepted so quickly during those two short visits.

Not only was I back on My Road to Viet Nam but I was determined to make it my last country of choice. In September, 2004, with plans made, housing secured, and Nate's higher education in mind, I attacked the first step in the plan, improve my language skills. Living in San Francisco offered a host of Vietnamese with whom I could practice the skills I had kept since my Army days. But 41 years after leaving had left a lot of vocabulary and syntax stuck in the back corners of my mind. I needed to, at the very least, improve my conversational and vocabulary skills.

Work wouldn't allow me enough time to meet with Vietnamese face to face. I needed some way to connect with them, especially those whose native language had been adapted to American living. The internet was my first thought to breaching that wall of vocabulary. Doing a Google search I found a number of websites for language skills improvement. I also discovered "Friendship" sites that offered direct contact with Vietnamese in Viet Nam. Some charged a fee, while others were free. Curious I signed up for one called "Asian-Euro". It was promoted to be a website where European/Caucasians can meet Asians to establish relationships online. The selection of "relationships" ranged from "practicing language" to "looking for a mate". The names, locations, a whole page of biographic details were included to help with selection. After putting my personal information online, I started searching for people who wanted to practice English and were not looking for any serious relationship! But on the other side of the coin, there were many requests coming to me requesting a connection as well. But not all were from Viet Nam. Men and Women from China, Philippines, and other Asian countries were looking for conversation to improve their English skills. Slowly, among the sincere requests to practice English, I was drawn into a web of solicitations and scams that became a near obsession.

For the remainder of 2004 I had a large number of "friends" from all over the Pacific rim countries. Some were the scam artists who were looking for "sugar daddies" to fund their life online. Among them were also good people in difficult situations who found that there were some who would listen to their problems. I was neither in a position nor an inclination to send money but I was ready and willing to offer suggestions and counseling conversations. I even met some friends in Shanghai who were interested in starting a Bible study online since their pastor was "old and not well educated in the Bible". I took their idea to our Baptist Missions Director. In the same way there were many people living in third world countries with needs, hopes, and dreams that intrigued me. Whether real or imagined was my challenge in understanding their needs as valid or simply scams for one reason or another. During 2005, my time online was reaching a peak. So much so that my wife had begun to resent the time I was spending online with other people, especially young women. In those days there was a woeful lack of older people who wanted to share and improve language skills.

Those days online began to affect my marriage. As I look back, I realize my marriage was already on the rocks but I managed to ignore the signs by staying busy with work, Nate, and being online. A marriage that grows cold or falls into a rut can easily be endangered by outside influences. Mine had shallow roots. I didn't notice it right away, but when I started to take an interest in moving to Viet Nam after the 2000 trip my wife was hesitant to accept that idea. When the 2004 trip ended and I began talking about the plans for moving to Viet Nam she firmly stood at not going. Her stand to stay was as strong as mine was to go. We were at a loggerhead where neither of us would budge. By the end of 2005, we were meeting with two church leaders of Valley Baptist Church to address her growing discontent with my activities online. Her accusations were getting more and more absurd as the meeting progressed. The decision from that meeting was that they would ask our State Baptist Convention for help. From that request came help that paid for eight weekly sessions with a Christian Counselor, Dr. Sam Leung, at the Christian Counseling Center in San Francisco. Those first sessions were hopeful and liberating for me but my wife refused to open herself up to revealing anything more than her accusations against me. By the eighth and final session, Dr. Leoung literally threw up his hands and proclaimed there was nothing he could do until we underwent individual counseling.

I have always been interested in knowing myself better. As Dr. Leoung told us that this would be an essential need for saving our marriage, I interpreted his frustration was with my wife because she would not look at herself and only pointed her finger at me. But individual counseling for me seemed like a very profitable endeavor considering I was preparing to move and retire in Viet Nam. Best to "know thyself" before making such a major shift in my life. After a few sessions with her counselor, I stopped paying for her $90 session and announced that she would have to pay for her own sessions. Meanwhile, I continued with my $100 sessions for my weekly insight to who I am. Through May that year I resolved a number of issues that helped me know and improve my life and the decisions that helped explain my behavior and attitudes that have perplexed me for many years. Not everything was resolved during that time. Some issues are still coming to light and resolution, but those sessions with him got me on the road to finding out who Michael Johnston is.

Stopping my sessions was more of an economic decision than a personal choice. By May, expenses had begun to mount up. Times together were almost exclusively trips to Indian casinos where we separated for night long sessions at slot machines. When I wasn't interested in going she would take one of the many $25 bus trips or a ride with her Uncle's family to the casinos just an hour or so from San Francisco or off to Reno early in the morning. My obsession with an online life while hers was the casino slots! Neither of us seemed willing to resolve a marriage that, in reflection, had died a long time before then. It was July 7, 2006 when she suddenly left the house in the car. Nate and I were home that afternoon when I heard a knock at the front door. A young woman was standing outside. When I opened the door she asked if I was Michael Ray Johnston! With some confusion at the question she handed a manila envelope to me. I took it. Immediately she turned around and left. Bewildered I closed the door and opened the envelope.

It was a summons to appear in court for a separation hearing. In the summons the particulars were that I turn over all the property to her and leave the premises. I interpreted that as a demand to give her what money and goods I had, and leave her and our son immediately. As I sat in the chair and wept, Nate came asking what happened. My only reply that I remember was "Your mother wants to put me out on the street and leave you with her. She wants to make me homeless.". My mind went to the death of my mother and the earlier passing of my sister. I felt like I had died along with them at their passing. Reading that summons made me feel like I was dying again. The stuff didn't matter to me. It was the demand for full custody of Nate that would take him away from me was my greatest fear and anger. I had no idea what to do. That day in court ended with the judge assigning a required mediation meeting before a hearing for separation could be decided. The date was set for mediation. At that meeting she had no bending at all. She, again, was not ready or willing to do anything but point her finger at me and ensure I would be gone, leaving only my money, our property, and our son with her. Everything I lived for was tied up in her demands. The mediator made her report to the Judge. When we returned to court the judge decided I would have to move out of the house with all my personal items by November 15, 2006.

My life had taken a seriously bad turn. I didn't think of it at the time but my road to Viet Nam had just been wrenched out of my hands. She got the house, the time share I had bought in Palm Springs, all of the household goods, and, the worst injury, full custody of Nate giving me only two hours of visitation a week. Twice a month he could stay over the weekend as long as he was returned to her by 6 p.m. Sunday evening. My Road to Viet Nam had come to an end. The hopes and dreams disappeared as I tried to figure out how I would pay off the debts to lawyers and creditors while paying $2000 a month for alimony and child support. That $100,000 annual income had dwindled in the process. Earlier that year, in June, I resigned as Pastor of Valley Baptist Church under the biblical principal that if a pastor can't manage his own household how could he manage a congregation of God's family. I had already left the House Church due to a member's constant disdain for paid clergy (from one member's discontent with his Catholic upbringing). All I had was my $6000 monthly salary from the City. 25% of that went to taxes. 30% of it went to her. 10% went to Insurance. Leaving me with enough for the 400$ monthly rent of a small room in the back of a garage in South San Francisco, a 50$ a month commute by train to work, and some food. By the end of the month I had about $10 discretionary for any other needs I might have. My hopes of retiring in Viet Nam had died. My job was slowly reduced to a cubicle creating exams for jobs with the City and County. My evenings were spent sitting in that little room watching TV and chatting with whomever was online.

Chapter 7 - The End of a Dream

The rest of 2006 was a dark time for me. That small room in the back of the old Ecuadorian lady's garage was an easy adjustment. It provided the solitude I needed to try to understand what had happened. In 2007, I was eventually brought into the light, but the beginning weeks continued to be very dark for me. I visited my doctor at Kaiser Health Care. He prescribed the anti-depressant, Prozac, for me. My hesitation to take the drug and my questions about how it would affect my depression was met with "you won't care about anything with that drug." I didn't want the symptoms ended, I wanted the cause to be resolved. I took the pills for a few weeks but felt the problems I was facing were still there. The pills ended and I sought another doctor. The Kaiser Health Care in South San Francisco had a mental health department. The doctor there invited me to attend a group therapy after she had interviewed me and scheduled a visit with the Meds Health Doctor. Neither of them felt the need for me to take medications. Therapy, she said, would address the reasons for my depression. Slowly I began to emerge from my darkness in the Spring of 2007. I started dating. But 34 years of marriage left me uncertain about being with other women. There were some highlights during that year of being alone. To control my depression my weekly visits with Nate helped a lot. Twice a month he was allowed to stay over the weekend. Thankfully, the one bright spot during 2007 was a friend, Guy Keenan, who was willing to help me out of my depression. A fellow computer programmer, he began inviting me to happy hour after work on Fridays. Along with another friend at DHR, Steve Martin, I began re-emerging into a single life with the speed of a turtle.

In August, 2007 I got permission to take Nate on a road trip up to Seattle. For two weeks my son and I drove up the coast and into the mountains of the American Northwest. Seattle, Tacoma, Portland were cities we got to visit. Mt. Rainer and other scenic routes we enjoyed together. Much like our times together in the cities and sites around San Francisco, my heart was temporarily cured from the depression I face back in my little room. It was Guy's generosity that got me back onto My Road to Viet Nam. What I learned in those therapy sessions was the reason I accepted Guy's offer and headed to Bangkok to meet

Jeanette in October. My Road to Viet Nam seemed to have taken a new route. Looking back after my return from the trip, I reasoned that maybe I was wrong about retiring in Viet Nam. Maybe Thailand was the true destination.

In August of 2007 I managed to get permission (it was hard for me to accept that I had to get permission) to take my son on a road trip. We headed up to Seattle, Washington. A Vietnamese friend I had met in June that year offered us a room to stay for the week. Walking around Seattle, talking with him about father and son things, and just enjoying a break from the worlds that kept us apart, was a welcomed relief.

In 2004 when I was searching for ways to improve my Vietnamese, I met Khanh Van online. She was a high schooler living in Saigon. Over the next few weeks became something of a daughter to me. I often call her my cyber-daughter. At the beginning of 2006 she moved to Seattle to attend a college to help her test out in English. I attended her graduation in June that year. When she visited me in South San Francisco, she helped with the loneliness. There were others I met through Van that helped as well. One of those friends was Linh who had recently moved from Viet Nam to San Francisco with her family. When we talked she knew I was missing the home life. In July, she introduced me to another Vietnamese, another new arrival. Her name is Thu. For a few weeks we were out and about in San Francisco almost daily. When she had to return to Atlanta, Georgia in August, once again, I had to rely on my weekly visits with Nate to hide my depression.

A Change in the Wind

On the morning of August 11, while Nate and I were on our road trip, I met a young woman on Skype. Nate's a late sleeper while I have always been an early riser. I let him know I would be out early the next morning looking for a coffee shop and go about my daily routine of coffee, Danish, news, and writing. When I turned my laptop on, it automatically signed in on Skype. That morning a window popped up with a simple "HI" in the message box. I'm not one to turn down a potential conversation. So, I responded. She said her name was "Jeanette". She is from the Philippines and had been living in Bangkok since 2006. We talked for a long time. When I got back to my South San Francisco garage room the following days began and ended with conversations with Jeanette. When I got back to my office, I shared my meeting Jeanette with a fellow friend and co-worker, Guy. Over time he saw my spirits lifted and my smile return after the year of brooding and sorrow. He asked me if I planned to visit her. With a bit of disappointment, I explained I had no money to travel. It was still going to my ex and creditors. He offered to pay my way if I made one promise to him. I had to promise him that I would return. I had no idea what he meant about that until some years later. When I made that promise to him, we went to a nearby ATM where he withdrew the cash and gave it to me. I booked the flight to Bangkok for the middle of October. It was a new beginning.

Months before, while I was still with my family, a serious tsunami devastated the coastal areas of Thailand. I was ready to volunteer to go help with recovery but finances wouldn't allow the trip for me. But my reasoning began to shape a new plan to replace the lost dream of Viet Nam. My mind justified the change as having short landed in Viet Nam when Thailand was surely the answer. Westerners were welcome there. Though its government was a monarchy, it should be better than the Communism that I had been taught while growing up in America. By end of October, 2007, I had a short term plan to resign my job with the City by the end of November and move to Thailand in January, 2008. It is one of those decisions I felt was the right one. Moving to Thailand was a bit tricky since the divorce wasn't final yet. But I felt that if I were to stay longer, my life would be over. I would be sunk into a quagmire of sorts just living from day to day. Nate would be turning 18 in 2008 and his child support would end. The alimony would be up to my ex and her lawyer to get it. With a little bit of cash in my pocket and a hope for a new future in my mind, I boarded the flight with hope and anticipation. That detour lasted seven years. Looking back, I remember meeting three Vietnamese in Bangkok. My Vietnamese they understood. Those brief meetings with them started my thinking about that dream I had so very long ago.

Overshot and landed in Thailand

It was a friend from my days of teaching at Thai Christian School. Jacques is a French Canadian who left his life in Thailand in 2010 for a new one in Viet Nam. In 2014 he invited me to join him in Pattaya, Thailand where he enjoyed vacationing from his work in Viet Nam. Through our conversations he further convinced me that I should visit him in Hanoi, Viet Nam. Looking for something to fill my time, since I had retired two years earlier, I accepted his second invitation. In April 2014 I made my first visit to Hanoi.

Stepping out of the airport terminal building I immediately felt at home. I looked up at a huge sign on the highway and realized I could read it! While in Thailand I was more often than not bewildered by the written language of the Thai. Now, back in a familiar land, I couldn't stop talking with the driver of the van that Jacques had ordered for me. The countryside, the weather, the language, everything about those 25 kilometers into Hanoi from the airport made me feel like I was coming home. For the first time in 45 years I felt like I was in the right place in the right time.

My Road to Viet Nam, whether I knew it then or not, was in the last mile. When I got back to Bangkok my first part of the plan was to approach Jeanette if she would like to visit Hanoi. That visit happened in December 2014. Both of us agreed that there seemed to be a better life waiting for us there. In July, 2015 almost all of our household in Bangkok was sold, given, or thrown away. 14 boxes and a bicycle we loaded in a truck to the airport in Bangkok. We were on our way to live in Viet Nam.

Epilogue

"For me to live is Christ..." Philippians 1:21

Early on that last morning in Bangkok, our entire seven years ended with 14 boxes and Jeanette's bicycle disassembled and wrapped piled in the back of the mover's pickup truck. The ride to Suvarnabumi Airport was full of laughter and conversation about the future, both for us. The glow of excitement from the two previous visits to Ha Noi still warmed our hearts as we made our first international move together.

My testimony as a Christian finally crystalized while listening to Dr. Joel Gregory deliver a message "The Power of Being a One Thing Person" based on this passage from Philippians, I realized for the most part that my life has been focused on that "one thing", to live is Christ. Through this book I have marveled at the things that I learned, came to understand, and adopted for my life were diverse and for the most part, unrelated-at the time-to the life I would live decades later. I still hang on to the love of my son, Nate, as the most significant gift in my life. But even before I became a Christian, God was working in my life. It was after that 10-year-old boy in Trinity Baptist Church in Shawnee, Oklahoma, at the side of my Grandma Johnston when I realized I had done things that were wrong (later to be known as "sin") that if I wanted to go to heaven, i.e. live through eternity with God, again a later understanding, I would and did make Jesus my Savior. Years later just before my baptism was scheduled, I additionally realized that He must be my Lord as well. That's the overarching philosophy of this book. My One Thing that has brought me this far, is my devotion to keeping Jesus as my Lord and Savior. That is to say God is my one thing that has given me power to be that One Thing Person.

For 65 years I walked this earth from shore to shore, crossed oceans, and climbed the mountains majesty. American the Beautiful was and still is an amazing nation. Our founding documents from the Declaration of Independence and our Constitution pull no punches that God has been the hope of our nation. This story has been about one man's journey through the best of times in America and through the some of the most difficult times of growth, change, and mysteries of living in a democracy.

But our founding fathers held one thing in common, whether by beliefs or by needs, they believed in God. They built my nation on the heart and soul of being one nation under God. Through the mistakes and misdirection over the years, my nation has struggled and grown to become a world power. It is the faith and belief that God is in charge of this world. And He is in charge of the lives of everyone, especially those who follow him through belief that his Son is the Savior. That's my story's premise.

God is in control, no matter how far we stray from his gift of faith. Within that context I look back over 42 of my 67 years and marvel at how He has guided me when I was at my worst. He has directed me when I was trying to be my best. He has protected me when I was in trouble and watched over me when I was down.

Above all, he has always been with me. Like the poem "Footprints in the Sand", he has never left me. My story is more about how God has directed my path despite who I am and how I have acted over all these years.

Being in Viet Nam has been an overriding hope in my mind since I was first introduced to this amazing country in 1970. My teachers in the Defense Language Institute's Biggs Field campus introduced me to the kind of people the Vietnamese are. Dedicated people in love with their homeland and committed to pursue peace at all costs. But more than being the dedicated warriors in a lifelong struggle for independence, they are a kind and friendly people.

As this story unfolded I have seen my life as a series of seven year cycles that are unique and under God's control. Within each cycle there have been experiences, knowledge, and skills that have lifted me to levels of human interaction that have become the rewards that I humbly look at as God's purpose for my life. Long ago, I realized I could not be much of a religious person, but I do have a strong sense that I am not completely in control of my life. God has been the source of my inspirations, hopes, and dreams. Through His consistent presence in my life, I have received accolades, awards, and appreciation for the work I felt like I had stumbled into. Reviewing the times of my life, especially on this Road to Viet Nam, I must and do give glory and praise to God for all that he has done in these seven decades of my life.

Credits

For years I have kept the stories of this book to myself. It has been a journey that took 45 years to come true I have scribbled notes over that time to weave this story together. But there are those that have made it my legacy and witness to God's will in my life. To see to the completion and distribution has been the woman that brought me out of depression. Jeanette Gengone Baclaan Johnston has stood beside me since January 2008. She has become my publisher, agent, and support in so many ways. Beside me for the last four years has been my Champion. My Son Nathanael, who moved from his hometown of San Francisco to build a new life in Tulsa. Our the twelve years we have been separated by the Pacific Ocean, he made the journey to bewith me as often as he could. Now we are only four miles apart. He has been my strength and my encouragement since the day I heard he was in his mother's womb. There are also many others from family and friends who have heard my story first hand. Of recent years, my sister, Sheryle, her daughter, Michele, my cousins Diane and Nancy who have shared encouragement with their help and prayers over the final years of this story. Friends from California, Texas, and Oklahoma and other parts of the States have been as much a part of my journey as well as friends who have lived their part in this story. Gary McCone, Andy Seel, Ron Whittaker and more from my Army days both in Language School and our time in the War in Viet Nam, have lived in my heart and mind through the rememorizes we have made. Those in San Francisco who understood me and lifted my spirits time after time. From Guy Keenan through the "Ladies of DHR" (Elizabeth, Maria, & Lyn) among many others at the Department of Human Resources have not only become life long friends, but also participants in this journey of mine.

Finally, the many people whom have crossed my path on the way to the fulfillment of this dream. Thank You All.